RAIL CENTRES:
DONCASTER

RAIL CENTRES:
DONCASTER

STEPHEN R. BATTY

LONDON
IAN ALLAN LTD

Contents

Title page left:
'V2' No 60923 heads north from Doncaster on 31 July 1963.
Eric Treacy

Title page right:
Class 45 No 45125 passes the old canal at Swinton. *A. Taylor*

British Library Cataloguing in Publication Data

Batty, Stephen R.
    Doncaster. - (Rail Centres)
    I. Title II. Series
    385.0942827

First published1991

ISBN 0 7110 2004 3

Published by Ian Allan Ltd, Shepperton, Surrey; and printed by Ian Allan Printing Ltd at their works at Coombelands, in Runnymede, England

Acknowledgements

Producing the text and illustrations for this book has given me endless opportunities for uncovering some long-forgotten pieces of railway history — including, perhaps, a few items of trivia, but gems none the less — and for ferreting around the countryside, searching out what is (or isn't) left of one and a half centuries of railway operation in an area which embraces all manner of landscapes from pit yard and goods yard to pasture and woodland. It has also given me not a few moments of anxiety, brought about by a sudden apparent lack of information on a particular topic or the non-existence of some badly-needed photographic material! Fortunately, Doncaster has been well-photographed and chronicled over the years, and many people have been particularly helpful in relieving my pangs. My greatest debt of thanks is due to Dr Arthur Barnett, for whilst doing some initial research into the history of the Doncaster coalfield I became distinctly aware of a sense of *déjà-vu* with regard to his excellent book *The Railways of the South Yorkshire Coalfield Since 1880*. Dr Barnett kindly allowed me to use his work as a source of reference, and I cannot thank him enough for doing so. His work is an unparalleled treasure-trove of information and has no equal, and must certainly be read by anyone wanting to follow the coalfield story more closely.

Many others have helped me in many ways. The staff of Doncaster Central Library and of Cusworth Hall Museum provided information via microfilm and exhibits; the Railway Correspondence & Travel Society allowed me to use the *Railway Observer* as a source of information; Trevor McKenna and Mario Hinchliffe provided journals and books; Bill Yeadon, the registrar of all LNER locomotive affairs, provided me with a ready-made (and much sought-after) allocation list; and Phil Robinson supplied an excellent set of maps and diagrams which he had drawn during his employment with BR.

I am grateful to all the photographers whose work appears in these pages, and several deserve a special word of thanks. Howard Turner has again delved into his collection and produced a set of prints, all of excellent quality and each with a particular memory attached. Tom Walker, late of Gresley House Control Office, loaned me a large collection of negatives and endless memorabilia such as correspondence, special notices and engine failure records etc. Mike Mitchell — the only 'quality' photographer who took it upon himself to record the colliery lines as much as possible before they disappeared — sent me a set of prints which will make any photographer of my generation long for his youth again. Peter Cookson, recorder of so much of the West Riding scene, provided me with some fine scenes on the ex-West Riding & Grimsby lines. Tony Goode, certainly one of Doncaster's best-known railway historians and indeed a Doncastrian by birth, supplied many photographs from his collection dating back to the later 1940s. Geoff Warnes provided views of the Dearne Valley Railway, and thought nothing of making a round trip of 40 miles by cycle to deliver them! Geoffrey Lewthwaite donated several of his station views of the area, and the staff of the NRM at York and Bill Stubbs of Alloa all did an excellent job of supplying archive material at short notice.

I must also thank the ladies who have been involved with yet another manuscript. My wife Andrea suggested the Doncaster title, and Mrs Jackie Robinson found me a typist in less than one minute flat via one very brief phone call. Mrs Maxine Robson then made an excellent job of my pages of scribble, barely using the Tippex brush (compared to my paint-brush technique) and showing what today's typewriters can really do. Perhaps modern technology isn't that bad after all.

Stephen R. Batty

March 1991

Introduction

With the high speeds which are now reached regularly on today's electrified East Coast main line, it is quite possible for the railway traveller largely to miss the surroundings which flash by the window as their train passes through Doncaster. What they surely would see, between blinks of the eyelids, is today's station and the famous Plant works nearby. Generations of enthusiasts have whiled away countless hours at the former and tramped away inches of shoe leather at the latter, all of which perhaps gives an unfair picture of the town's railway history. Doncaster's railway development involved far more than simply building a station on the King's Cross-Edinburgh line and then constructing a large railway workshop nearby; coal mining was the prime mover behind the town's growth, and the spread of this industry and the associated expansion of railways have given the area a fascinating history.

At the dawn of the railway age Doncaster was a quiet, genteel rural town with an economy which depended entirely on agricultural produce and trade brought in by the Great North Road. A navigable waterway had been built to transfer goods and materials, and there was neither the need nor the interest to build any railway to the town. The picture changed when the Barnsley coal owners needed a better means of taking their coal to either London or the Humber for export, and when one far-sighted railway promoter succeeded in bringing the Great Northern Railway, complete with workshops, to Doncaster. This was followed by the development of the Doncaster coalfield and the early era of the 'super-pit', and by 1914 the transformation was complete — agriculture had been replaced by the coal and railway industries. Over the years since then, both have been trimmed down radically, but both are still with us. The Barnsley coalfield has virtually disappeared and the Doncaster pits have been greatly reduced in number, but the survivors are still feeding coal traffic to BR for supply to the area's power stations. The main line has finally been electrified, 35 years after the idea was first considered seriously, and BR's principal passenger-carrying money-earner has been turned into a showcase railway. Even when the social and technological changes which have taken place generally across the country during the last 150 years are borne in mind, Doncaster's experience of these trends covers the widest possible field of events.

1: Origins

Doncaster is a small town in South Yorkshire which straddles the river Don, the old Great North Road and British Rail's electrified East Coast main line from King's Cross to Edinburgh. These arteries of transport point directly to the town's principal source of livelihood from Roman times to the middle of the 19th century, when the arrival of railways began the series of changes which eventually developed Doncaster into an industrial outpost at the south-eastern corner of the West Riding of Yorkshire. In the closing years of the 20th century much of this industry has been changed greatly by events of the past ten years, whereas the importance of railway connections and the decline of road and water transport continue to reflect a chain of events set in motion 150 years ago.

Twixt Factories and Farms

Doncaster lies on the boundary between the industrial zones to the west and the agricultural areas to the east, a position which even today is reflected in the approaches by road and in the appearance and feel of the town itself. Entry from Wakefield, Barnsley or along the Don valley from Sheffield and Rotherham is a distinctly post-industrial experience, whereas the roads from Haxey, Bawtry or Worksop bring rural scenery to the very edge of the town. The Doncaster coalfield was not exploited until the last years of the 19th century, and during the mid-1800s, it was mining in the Barnsley and Wakefield areas that fuelled the industrial furnaces of Lancashire and Yorkshire and also provided a local export from these coalfields to other parts of the country, especially London and the south. Thus in the early years of railway development between 1830 and 1850, Doncaster was a truly agricultural market town, with the nearest industrial manufactory towns some miles away to the west, and the great farmlands of Lincolnshire stretching away to the east and south-east, with the vast Fens lying beyond towards Boston and East Anglia. Northwards lay the fertile Vale of York and the river Ouse, and southwards was the still rural Nottinghamshire, where coalfield development was decades into the future. During the early 19th century the ancient borough of Doncaster depended for its considerable prosperity upon the regular markets, the trade brought along the Great North Road between London and Scotland and also by the large network of connecting coach services, and upon the annual race meeting held every September.

Some manufacturing was established by this time, but only on a small scale for the production of iron, agricultural machinery and ropes. In 1787 the Reverend Edmund Cartwright had caused a little local difficulty by introducing machine-operated muslin and calico mills, thereby causing considerable amounts of smoke and unwanted smells to be discharged on the town. He became extremely unpopular with the townspeople and the town's corporation, and after several threats of destruction he closed the plant and departed in 1820, leaving the textile production of Doncaster in the hands of the many local producers (at the time) of knitted stockings. One wonders how the iron foundry and machinery works managed to stay environmentally acceptable!

Doncaster was famous for the number and quality of the markets held in the town throughout the year. Although no covered area was provided at this time, the markets were always well-attended and made a great deal of money for the corporation. The Saturday corn market regularly saw up to 10 bargeloads being despatched to Sheffield along the river Don, and a wool market was held on the same days from mid-June to early August, ending with a Wool Fair. Fish was another popular commodity, with salmon from Newcastle and Carlisle, sea fish from Flamborough and the Lincolnshire coast, and river fish from Gamston, in Nottinghamshire, all being traded. Cattle, horses and sheep were sold too, with particular fairs being held in February and November.

Excellent communications, fertile land and the availability of a wide range of first-class provisions made Doncaster into a town of great gentility and elegance which boasted many families of great wealth among its population. One commentator of the time stated:

'...from the beauty of the town, the salubrity of the air, the goodness of the roads and the delightful promenades, Doncaster may perhaps vie with any other town in the Kingdom as a most desirable residence not only for the affluent, but more particularly for persons of small fortune.'

The Races

Such gentility and elegance were focused particularly upon the horse races held during September of each year, when the town would almost burst at the seams with racegoers and holidaymakers who converged on

Left:
A barge moored alongside St George's Church, Doncaster, about 1899. The original church was destroyed by fire in 1853, and the later structure was designed by Sir Gilbert Scott between 1854-1858.
National Railway Museum (NRM) (DON167)

the week-long meeting and swelled the coffers of the innkeepers, tradesmen, market traders and the corporation to an extent which was the envy of racing towns across the country. Horse racing in the town dated from 1703, when the corporation voted a four-guinea subscription towards the cost of a plate for the winner of a race on the Moor. Rarely can such a modest civic investment have yielded such long-term benefits. The famous St Leger race was instituted in 1776, and a stand was built at the racecourse in 1825 with the proceeds of 30 guinea (£31.50) subscriptions raised from the nobility and gentry. A four-day meeting was held during the third week of September, but this was increased to five when the stand was opened. The meeting was one of the principal social events in the land, with many families from north and south attending, and *all* the country aristocracy from South Yorkshire, Nottinghamshire and Lincolnshire being present. For five hectic days the race-goers could hunt in the morning, watch the races in the afternoon, and spend the evening at a ball, the theatre, or gambling instead.

Passenger travel to this bygone Doncaster was based entirely upon the horse. Until the end of the 1830s, Doncaster lay at the centre of a stage-coach network which radiated from the town to all points of the compass and which connected with the Great North Road traffic. Whereas today's A1 road traffic is mercifully kept clear of the town by virtue of the Doncaster by-pass, the original road entered from Retford and Bawtry before leaving towards Ferrybridge. Doncaster's principal hostelries were the Old Angel Inn, the New Angel Inn and the Rein Deer Inn, and between them they handled seven four-horse and 20 two-horse coaches, nine stage-waggons and 100 horses for posting, making a total of 258 horses. The stage coaches were keenly-timed and well-kept, but the mail coaches were the real flyers of the day, averaging 10mph including stops. A contemporary view

of the town's horse-powered activity stated 'The private travelling carriages and post-chaises were also well-horsed, and the post-boys were active, and neat in their attire. These, together with the stage-waggons, with their elephantine horses, the sets-out of the commercial traveller, the carriages of the neighbouring families, the gigs and private horses, made the town quite alive.'

Enter the Railway

Doncaster's coach network was slightly affected by the opening of the Leeds & Selby Railway in 1834 and of the York & North Midland Railway in 1839, but the hammer-blow came in June 1840 with the opening of the North Midland Railway, giving a rapid 217-mile journey between Leeds and London along a railway which passed by Doncaster at Swinton, easily accessible by coach and/or water transport. Even though a direct railway to London through the eastern counties was a decade away, Stephenson's NMR finished the long-distance coach trade from the capital to the Midlands and North at one blow. Many cross-country services survived for a few years into the 1840s, particularly in the relatively rail-less east, but the second 'Railway Mania' from 1845 saw the stage and mail coaches consigned to history. By 1844 the Old Angel Inn had closed, and the remaining two inns could muster only 60 horses between them.

If the railways were seen to kill off quickly the town's principal road transport industry, then events concerning navigation along the river Don took a rather different turn. The river rose high in the Pennines above Penistone and flowed into two outlets, meeting the Aire at Rawcliffe, near Goole, and the Trent at Adlingfleet. From these two mouths navigation had been possible, under favourable conditions, as far as Doncaster since time immemorial, but commercial development of the river into an important waterway began during the reign of King Charles I. The great Dutch engineer Vermuyden was given the job of draining Hatfield Chase and so making available large areas of land for agricultural use. This was done to the satisfaction of the Hatfield landowners, but unfortunately the scheme caused severe flooding at Fishlake, Sykehouse and Snaith which ultimately led to local rioting in 1628. Five years later a new course for the river was cut from Newbridge to Goole at a cost of £30,000, solving the flooding problem at a stroke. The new cut— Dutch River, as it is called today — was wide and straight and diverted the flow away from the two original outlets, which quickly silted up. Traces of these are still shown on today's Ordnance Survey maps.

River Traffic

Tidal waters reached Doncaster and large vessels could reach Fishlake or Thorpe-in-Balne all the year round. These could actually reach the town if a flood tide was flowing, but Doncaster's river traffic consisted mostly of smaller boats which could operate generally for about nine months of the year. No vessel could penetrate any further upstream, and transport to and from Rotherham and Sheffield depended on the roadways. Moves followed to make the river more navigable, to allow vessels to reach Sheffield and also to ensure the larger boats could reach Doncaster at all times. In 1694 a Bill was promoted to this end, which was backed by many West Riding interests, including Leeds corporation, and also by Sir Godfrey Copley of Sprotborough, who had interests with the Aire & Calder Navigation. However, landowners feared that such improvements would cause flooding, the mill owners of Sheffield and Doncaster were worried about water supplies, and some commercial interests thought a better river (or canal) would result in Don-

caster being effectively by-passed, and they successfully opposed the Bill. This was a great pity and a great opportunity lost, for not many years passed before those who opposed the Bill realised that the river simply *had* to be improved in order to give access for the increasingly large quantities of raw materials, finished products and agricultural produce which the markets were demanding. By the time Doncaster corporation had seen the light and produced its own Bill for improvements — backed also by Sheffield and Barnsley — in 1704, the opposition had united with sufficient strength to defeat the Bill. Several further defeats followed and it was not until 1726 that any real progress was made. A Sheffield-promoted Bill was passed for improvements from Tinsley to Holmstile, three-quarters of a mile downstream from Doncaster, and in the following year a further Act was gained for improvements to be made onwards to Wilsick House at Thorpe-in-Balne. The two undertakings responsible for the navigation of the river, based in Sheffield and Doncaster, were amalgamated in 1731 by an Act which also included provisions for improving the final stretch from Wilsick House to the river Ouse at Goole. In 1733 the Company of the Proprietors of the Navigation of the River Dun was established, many more improvements were laid out for the Sheffield end of the system, and 13 locks — including those at Barnby Dun and Kirk Sandall — were to be built. Plans were also

Below:
As well as being placed astride the Great North Road, Doncaster benefited from the navigable river Don, which provided a waterway from Sheffield to the Humber. An HST set forming the 08.10 Edinburgh-Newquay crosses the river at Conisbrough on 28 July 1990 *S. R. Batty*

laid for the removal of three bridges over the Dutch River, but these were thwarted by landowners and resulted in any further progress along this length of the Navigation being dependent upon dredging work. More work followed in 1740 when the channel was widened from Wilsick to Bramwith and a long cut was made near Stainforth, eliminating some of the wilder meanderings of the river in the area. The end result was a 33 mile navigation from Tinsley, near Sheffield, to Stainforth, including 17 locks before the tidal reach of the Don was encountered. Thorne became a shipping point from Hull, with keel boats reaching here via the Humber and the Dutch River. Vermuyden's waterway continued to be hampered by the three bridges, which also limited the size of any boats built at Thorne to about 400 gross tons.

The latter years of the 18th century saw the Navigation prospering with the carriage of goods to the much-improved Tinsley wharves and a good cutter service for passengers plying between London and Thorne. The 'Canal Mania' saw the company involved with plans for the Barnsley canal, the Dearne & Dove and the Stainforth & Keadby, all of which were built, but plans for extending the Navigation into Sheffield under a 1792 scheme failed. Passenger services thrived until the railway age finally dawned on the area, and in 1806 the sailing packet *Nelson* was operating a twice-weekly service between Thorne and Hull. By 1816, steam power had arrived, the *Britannia* being one of a fleet of several steamboats, and in 1818 a thrice-weekly service was operating with a coach connection to and from Doncaster,

which was eventually extended to Sheffield in 1820. The last major improvements to the Navigation in this pre-railway era took place by virtue of an Act of 1821 and involved making three new cuts at Arksey, Long Sandall and Barnby Dun. These were surveyed and built by George Leather and were completed by late 1823. Leather was a leading figure in many West Riding railway promotions, particularly in the Leeds and Sheffield areas, and his far-sightedness and understanding of transport needs and problems left him in no doubts about the future of canals and railways. Far from wanting to oppose the spread of railways, Leather saw mutual advantages for both canal and railway owners if only the two could work together. He pressed for further improvements to be made, including the cutting of a new canal from Stainforth to Goole which would allow much better movement of coal to either the new port here (opened in 1826) or for shipping along the Humber to Hull and thence to London. Thorne wharf fell into disuse at this time, the large tonnages of Barnsley's coal and Doncaster's agricultural produce sailing directly to Goole. In 1831 the Navigation was asked by the Rochdale Canal Co to join with them in general oppo-

Below:
The river has been navigable to the east of the town since time immemorial. A loaded coal barge sails eastwards as a Class O4 2-8-0 returns to Doncaster with an early trial run of coal wagons from Thorpe Marsh power station.
T. S. Walker

sition to *all* future railway schemes, but the Dun Company was too clever to become embroiled in such a hopeless cause. The coal and the corn had to be transported for shipment, and the Navigation company fully intended to keep this lucrative traffic, regardless of whether railways were involved.

As late as 1836, plans were made for more improvements between Doncaster and the Ouse, this time involving the owners of the Stainforth & Keadby Canal of 1793. The Dun Navigation offered to buy out the smaller company but disagreements amongst the shareholders saw the entire scheme lost. The S&K shareholders must have regretted this lost opportunity when they eventually did sell out in 1849, at a far lower price than the Dun company had offered 13 years earlier. The opening of the North Midland Railway in June 1840 gave the company a chance of much better business along the waterway not only by carrying coal from Swinton, but also by ferrying passengers between the railway and Doncaster. A new cut was started in 1842 to take the canal nearer to the town centre, and two years later an agreement for transferring traffic was reached with the Sheffield & Rotherham Railway. By the start of the second 'mania' in 1845 the Navigation was actively seeking a sound railway partner from amongst the many

schemes being put forward at the time, and they eventually made approaches to the South Yorkshire Coal Railway. Hopefully, this would give rail access along the Blackburn valley towards the Barnsley coalfield, and yield lucrative business along the way to Hull. Opposition from the Aire & Calder Navigation sunk the scheme however, but eventually the Dun Company pacified its powerful neighbour and the amalgamation Act was successfully passed in July 1847. By this time the SYCR had joined with the Goole, Doncaster, Sheffield & Manchester Junction Railway and was blessed with the thankfully short title of the South Yorkshire, Doncaster & Goole Railway. One condition of the Act stated that amalgamation would only take place when half the railway company's capital had been raised and spent, and this took place by April 1850.

This, then, was the situation at Doncaster in the years immediately prior to, and during the early stages of, railway development of the town. Prosperity was ensured by a thriving local economy based on agriculture and a healthy road-travel business, and wealth and gentility abounded in one of the kingdom's most favoured towns. Prior to 1840 there was no local interest in railway promotion whatsoever, and the Dun Navigation was making a very profitable business out of transporting raw materials and agricultural produce to markets near and far. Doncaster could have been left 'out in the cold' for far longer, but events took a different turn due mainly to the efforts of one man who saw where the town's future could lie.

Below:
A Class 142 DMU crosses the river at Long Sandall, close by the lock on the Don Navigation. *S. R. Batty*

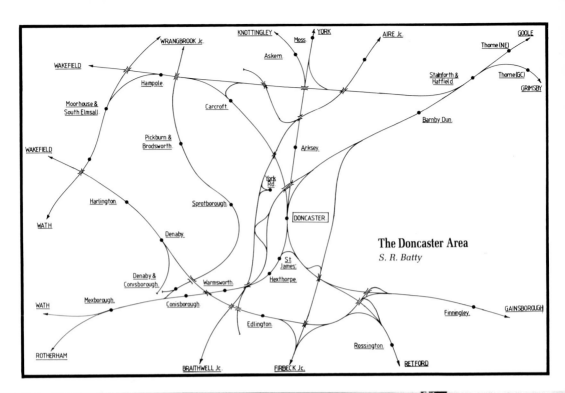

The Doncaster Area

S. R. Batty

Bawtry could have become a railway crossroads if some early plans had succeeded. Here Class A4 No 60009 *Union of South Africa* passes with the up 'Elizabethan' on 1 July 1955. *L. Overend*

2: The Railways Reach Doncaster

The Origins of the GNR

Doncaster's early railway history can be conveniently broken into three separate developments:

   1 Connecting the Barnsley coalfield with Thorne, Goole and Hull.
   2 Access to the industrial West Riding via Wakefield.
   3 Constructing a main line from London to the north.

All these plans ultimately came to fruition within a very short space of time, but whereas the first two were accomplished in a relatively straightforward manner, the third took 25 years to appear in its final form and often looked as if it would bypass Doncaster completely. As early as 1827 a survey was made for a London-Lincoln-York railway which avoided the town, but this scheme did not prosper and nothing more was heard of it. It did, however, favour the so-called 'Fens' line via Cambridge, Boston and Lincoln, as against later alternatives routed via Peterborough, Grantham and Retford, known later as the 'Towns' line. Further schemes were drawn up by 1835/36 for a railway to York, with the Northern & Eastern Railway wanting a route via Cambridge, Peterborough and Lincoln and the infant Great Northern Railway planning to run through Cambridge and Lincoln only. Both schemes were lost in Parliament in favour of the North Midland Railway, which eventually reached York in 1840 by a longer route which served many large centres of population such as Rugby, Derby and Sheffield. The Fens line schemes were resurrected briefly before 1840, but no progress was made and the first railway 'mania' then died out as economic conditions across the country hardened in the face of a recession.

In 1843 another railway scheme appeared, to reach York from London via Lincoln and Thorne and also missing Doncaster by several miles to the east. Known as the Direct Northern Railway, this scheme was also influenced by the Manchester & Leeds Railway Co's desire to extend its own system eastwards by building on from Wakefield to Doncaster, Lincoln and Boston, so perpetuating the Fens line plan. Meanwhile, the Towns line idea had gained some favour with those parties still pushing for a direct London-York line, and in 1844 the two schemes of 1835/36 were combined as the London & York Rail-

way running via Peterborough and Grantham but then swinging eastwards via Sleaford to reach Lincoln and Gainsborough. At this point the West Riding MP, Edmund Denison, stepped into matters and campaigned successfully with Samuel Hughes, a promoter of the schemes of the mid-1830s, to have the London & York's line diverted westwards through his home town of Doncaster. George Hudson's route from London to the centre of his empire at York was now clearly threatened, as the London and York was some 30 miles shorter. Hudson used whatever tactics he could think of to get the new railway thrown out of Parliament, and resorted to promotion of several alternative lines which would have stopped the London & York dead. He campaigned furiously wherever possible, and eventually succeeded by questioning some of the small print in the new company's money-raising schemes. It was a minor technicality, but it was enough to get the Bill thrown out and give Hudson some breathing space. The Direct Northern plans were also thrown out, but Hudson knew it was only a matter of time before a direct London-York railway was built on the eastern side of the country. And well he might have feared it, as it would undoubtedly offer higher speed and better running compared to the Midland Railway's profitable but congested route via the heart of England. Hudson was desperate to prevent the new railway for as long as possible and lost no time in belittling the promoters, saying they would run out of money before even reaching Grantham, challenging them to speed contests from London to York, and even casting doubts on the legality of their capital-raising means. He may indeed have been a very able railway promoter driven by strong personal ability and business drive, not to say greed, but one wonders if his outpourings against the London & York were even rational. Edmund Denison, on the other hand, was known and respected for his integrity and strength of character, and Hudson's bile left him completely unmoved, save for feelings of utter contempt for his rival.

During 1846 the London & York amalgamated with the Direct Northern Railway to become the Great Northern Railway, running from London to York via Peterborough, Newark, Retford and Doncaster, with a loop from Peterborough through Boston and Lincoln back to the main line at Bawtry. Cambridge and Leeds were to be reached as soon as possible after the main line was built, resulting eventually in a successful combination of both 'Towns' and 'Fens' lines being built. This time the promotion was successful, and the Act was passed on 26 June 1846. Capital of £5.6million was needed, a truly massive sum for the times, in addition to the vast expense incurred in getting the Bill through Parliament due to opposition from the London & North Western Railway, the Midland Railway, the Eastern Counties Railway and many landowners.

There were plans for branches from Arksey to Wakefield and from Bawtry to Sheffield, but these were rejected in the Act. This eventually caused no difficulty as alternative access to these places was gained. The Wakefield, Pontefract & Goole Railway (WPG), a protégé of the Manchester and Leeds, was authorised in July 1846 to build a branch from Knottingley to meet a short spur off the GNR main line near Askern, so reaching Wakefield via the M&LR line. Sheffield was ultimately reached by using running powers over the Manchester, Sheffield & Lincolnshire Railway's line from Retford, but the loss of the Bawtry-Sheffield branch had repercussions for the planned Lincoln loop. After losing the branch the GNR decided to bring the loop back to the main line at Rossington, but strong fox-hunting interests prevented two attempts at this alteration from getting through Parliament! After the last failure, in 1848, the GNR negotiated with the MSLR for further use of its planned Retford-Lincoln line instead of building the northern end of the loop, and Bawtry's planned railway crossroads disappeared forever.

The Lancashire and Yorkshire Railway

The GNR's running powers over the WPG Askern-Knottingley branch not only allowed the GNR to reach Wakefield, but also brought it within a stone's throw of Leeds by using similar powers granted by the Lancashire & Yorkshire Railway (as the M&LR became during 1847) to Methley Junction, on the North Midland Railway. In return, the GNR was to allow the LYR running powers into its Doncaster station. Enter once more George Hudson, who now decided to try and divert the Great Northern traffic into York via his own system. This he did craftily by exploiting the GN's weak financial position, for no revenue was yet being earned and the company still had not recovered fully from the expensive Parliamentary battle of 1846. Hudson built a short connecting spur from Knottingley, on the LYR line, to Burton Salmon on his own ex-York & North Midland Railway, and offered to allow the GNR to use this for access to York (via Milford and Church Fenton) if it would drop its own plans for a line from Doncaster to York. Although the GNR board was extremely reluctant to embrace Hudson after their troubles since 1844, the company's financial state was not good and the savings produced by not building its own line to York were considerable, and the agreement went

ahead. Hudson also granted running powers from Methley into Leeds, which gave the company access to an area which it, and subsequently the London & North Eastern Railway and then British Railways, served well. Its own line thus terminated at an end-on junction with the LYR branch at Askern Junction, a situation which prompted the often-quoted remark from the GN chairman, Denison, that their main line ended '...in a ploughed field four miles north of Doncaster.'

Construction of the Knottingley branch went ahead promptly and no engineering difficulties were encountered. The opening of the line was fixed for Monday 5 June 1848, from its junction with the LYR at Knottingley through to Stockbridge station on the GNR line, beyond Askern Junction. (Stockbridge was renamed Arksey & Stockbridge from December 1850, and again renamed to plain Arksey from September 1854.) A service of horse-drawn omnibuses ran from the Angel Inn at Doncaster to the station at Stockbridge, and a procession of the carriages and gigs of the local gentry set off at 10.30. Unfortunately, the first train was already well-filled by the time the Doncastrians arrived, people having converged from the local villages and hamlets of Arksey, Bentley, Tilts and Shaftholme. Somehow, everyone was crammed into the 15 coach train and the two locomotives set off amidst much cheering from the assembled crowds along the way and the pealing of church bells. The GN/LYR junction in Reedholme Wood was clearly defined by the different colours of ballast used by the two companies. More passengers joined at Askern, and Lord Hawke boarded at Womersley for the journey through to Pontefract. Typical summer weather was encountered when the passengers travelling in the open wagons were given a soaking during a hailstorm. Knottingley was a truly rural place then, with the smell of lime-burning being noted and the clear views of Hemingbrough church, 'Hambleton Haugh' and 'Brayton Barf' being remarked upon. Pontefract was reached at midday, but the town was completely unprepared for the sudden arrival of so many people and supplies of food and drink were hard to find. After looking round the town and castle, the passengers returned to the station for a 14.00 departure — the total number was estimated at over 700 people. (A further return trip ran later in the day, but no comment was made in the press reports regarding the

WOMERSLEY STATION.

NORTON

effect on Pontefract of this second wave of visitors!) Arrival at Stockbridge at 14.45 was followed by a mad rush for carriages and omnibuses for the ride into Doncaster, but many ended up walking. Meanwhile, 400 navvies were regaled with roast beef and ale at Askern, Womersley, Knottingley 'and other places on the line' by the contractors, Micklethwaite & Son. The public service commenced on the following day, and a Doncaster-Wakefield timetable was published:

Dep Doncaster (by Omnibus): 07.05 08.25 12.05 15.10 16.45
Dep Wakefield: 09.05 11.25 14.35 17.10 07.05

A service to and from York was provided by omnibuses between Knottingley and Burton Salmon, on the YNMR route from Normanton to York. These omnibuses left Knottingley after the arrival of the 08.25 and 16.45 departures from Doncaster, and in the reverse direction they left Burton Salmon after the arrival of the 09.50 and 14.45 departures from York, thus connecting into the 11.25 and 17.10 trains from Wakefield to Doncaster. These services lasted until Hudson's Knottingley-Burton Salmon curve was opened in April 1850, and thus Doncaster's first railway service depended on horse-drawn transport, to a greater or lesser degree, for almost two years.

Ready for the Races

Having reached Stockbridge by June 1848, the LYR's new principal aim was to work through to the completed Doncaster station in time for the September race week. Work proceeded rapidly, and a train was

Right:
The ECML exit south from Doncaster station has changed greatly in recent years. Class A3 No 60105 *Victor Wild* gets away past Garden sidings with the 12.35 Leeds (Central)-King's Cross on 15 April 1955. *P. J. Lynch*

This picture:
Over 20 years later, Class 47 No 47407 passes sidings full of mgr wagons near the much-reduced motive power depot with an up express on 28 May 1977. *L. A. Nixon*

sent into the town on 11 August, consisting of a string of earth wagons which had been temporarily fitted-out with rudimentary seats and attached to a contractor's locomotive by the name of *Irwell*. Some ringing of church bells was done, but no great ceremony took place. As September drew nearer — the St Leger was to be run on the 13th — the LYR's confidence grew and the company declared the station would be open from Thursday 7 September. Some had hoped for an opening by the first day of the month, but the station would not have been ready at this time and the LYR did not want to risk any bad publicity for the sake of one week's work. Notices were published advertising race specials from Manchester (Victoria) at 07.00, travelling via Pontefract and arriving at Doncaster at 11.15, and one from Halifax (07.00) via Leeds (07.50) to arrive at approxi-

mately 10.00. Further trains would leave Goole at 07.30 and 09.00 and York at 06.00, 07.25 and 09.50. Return travel, however, was not planned so meticulously — the LYR merely stated that return trains would be '...despatched as often as may be practicably convenient to the company between 5.30pm and 7.30pm'. The LYR always preferred goods traffic to passenger business along its West Riding lines! Taken to an extreme, this little statement almost implies that the company was outraged to discover that having despatched passengers by a timetabled service, they were now obliged to *return* them to their originating station as promptly as possible!

Doncaster station was duly inspected by two LYR directors, William Moxon of Pontefract and Mr Bateson of Leeds, and also by Mr Cawkwell, (Goods Department Superintendent), Edmund Denison,

(GNR Chairman), Mr Carr, (Resident Engineer of the GNR), and a Mr Tate of Peto & Betts, contractors. Captain Winn performed the government inspection of the line and left the station on the afternoon of the 5th, but for some unknown reason the public service started on Friday 8 September, one day later than anticipated. The first train departed for Knottingley at 07.30 and the first arrival took place at 10.30, all without any ceremony apart from a band playing at various times of the day for some of the trains. Railway operation during St Leger week was a great success with 30,000 people travelling *daily* and 24 uniformed policemen being deployed at the station.

The South Yorkshire Railway

This character of a railway was promoted in order to connect the Barnsley coalfield with railway and water outlets to the coal markets of the south, and initially Doncaster did not play any great part in these plans. Similar railways were projected during the depressed years of the early 1840s, but all had failed. Nevertheless the South Yorkshire Coal Railway prospectus was issued in late 1845, and proposed building a railway from a junction on the Huddersfield & Sheffield Junction Railway, near Shepley, to go via Barnsley, Wath and Mexborough to Rossington on the planned GNR line. A connecting spur was to reach Doncaster directly, but the prime object was to gain access to the southbound main line at Rossington. The Dun Navigation Company supported the scheme, as mentioned earlier, but the opposition of the Aire & Calder Company and also that of many other projected railways of the same period saw the railway lost in Parliament. During 1846 the SYCR amalgamated with one of these companies, which had contributed to the plan's downfall and then jointly prepared a further Bill for the Parliamentary session of 1847. This merging with the Goole, Doncaster, Sheffield & Manchester Junction Railway produced a new title of the South Yorkshire, Doncaster &

Goole Railway, which was an accurate description of the company's ambitions.

Thus by 1847, Doncaster was assured of a place on the railway map by virtue of all the schemes — some under way, some unstarted and some destined only for oblivion — then being bandied about in the rush following the second 'mania'. On 4 January Robert Milner, the Mayor, held a public meeting at the Mansion House to discuss the various projects and their effect upon the town. Discussion amongst the 135 who attended quickly settled upon three features, the proposed SYDGR, the GNR and the Dun Navigation Co. As Doncaster corporation had shares to the value of £24,000 in the Navigation company, it naturally wanted to protect its investment. However, a rival proposal to the SYDGR, the Sheffield, Barnsley, Doncaster and Goole Railway, had offered to buy out the corporation's shares in the face of a similar (but better) proposal from the SYDGR. The Sheffield company was a protégé of the Midland Railway, but the meeting felt was too remote to be of any real use to the town, whereas the SYDGR and the Navigation company clearly had plans for mutual improvement and development which would maintain the values of the canal and the wharves. Some concern was expressed at the power of a railway and canal monopoly, but the meeting voted resoundingly in favour of the SYDGR scheme and against the Midland-backed SBDGR.

One interesting point raised concerned the good relationship between the proposers of the railway and the GNR, several of those at the meeting hoping that this might encourage the GN to build its planned railway works in the town. At this time, the GN's Act was only six months old, and the arrival of the railway works — the Plant — was some six years away.

As a result of careful lobbying support was gained from the GNR and from the coal owners, the Aire & Calder Co was successfully pacified, and the SYDGR received its Act on 22 July 1847. Charles Bartholomew was appointed Engineer, a position he

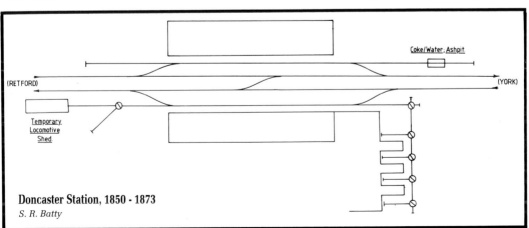

Doncaster Station, 1850 - 1873

S. R. Batty

19

also held on the Dun Navigation Co, and the first sod was cut at Levitt Hagg, Warmsworth, on 1 March 1848. Construction to Swinton, on the North Midland Railway, took 20 months and was described at the time as passing through a beautifully picturesque part of South Yorkshire with '. . . level surface, sloping meadow, stubborn rock and huge mountain.'

The first trip along the line left Doncaster at 10.00 on Saturday 20 October 1849, the train consisting of two Midland Railway first class saloons and one Great Northern Railway truck which had been temporarily fitted out with seats. A small South Yorkshire ballast locomotive propelled the stock out of the station without any form of ceremony being held, and the passengers included Denison, the GNR chairman, his son Edmund Beckett Denison, Robert Baxter, Edmund Baxter, Sir Isaac Morley of the Midland Railway, and Charles Bartholomew.

For a relatively short railway the SYR certainly included plenty of notable engineering features on the way to Swinton. Warmsworth cutting was (and still is) a very deep, narrow slot made through solid rock for every foot of its 70ft depth, and the well-cut stonework and several retaining walls built into the cutting were gazed upon with admiration, whilst the correspondent of the *Doncaster Gazette* waxed lyrical about the 'Herculean labours of the hardy sons of toil' who had used nothing more than pick, shovel and wheelbarrow (plus a little black powder) during the construction. A three-ribbed, 600-ton iron bridge carried the line over the Don, and Foulsyke tunnel brought the train in view of Conisbrough castle.

Continuing the journey, Sir Joseph Copley joined the train shortly before arrival at Swinton, where a brief inspection was made of the works being carried out to take the line under the MR towards Barnsley. A return journey to Doncaster was made in 23 minutes, followed by a directors' meeting and dinner at the Angel Inn. The government inspection was made on 31 October and public opening followed on 10 November, using a station in Cherry Tree Lane which lay south-westwards of the GNR station and was connected to that company's main line by north- and south-facing spurs. The former ran on from Cherry Tree Lane station to meet the main line at Doncaster South Junction, i.e. facing northwards, and the latter left the GN line at Doncaster Bridge Junction and curved south-westwards to meet the SYR line at St James's Junction. The GNR was keen to do business with the South Yorkshire and built parts of these spurs itself — the north-facing spur used GNR metals from a point halfway between the SYDGR and GNR stations, and a similar arrangement existed on the south-western connection. Stations were provided at Hexthorpe, Sprotborough and Conisbrough, but only the latter was ready at the public opening — the first

Above:
Class 45 No 45125 heads the 09.50 Newcastle-Poole over the Don Navigation near Swinton on 6 August 1983. *A. Taylor*

Left:
Warmsworth cutting was hailed as a triumph of manual labour at its opening in 1849. This is the 07.15 Newcastle-Paignton threading its way through the 70ft depth on 28 July 1990. *S. R. Batty*

Above:
The 06.48 Cardiff-Newcastle passes Warmsworth quarry and approaches the cutting on 28 July 1990. *S. R. Batty*

Left:
Two Class 31 locomotives haul coal empties out of the cutting and past Warmsworth signal box towards Conisbrough on 11 August 1970. *T. G. Flinders*

Right:
St James' Bridge station, thronged with young train spotters on the right, on 19 July 1958. *J .H. Turner collection*

two were delayed until 1 February 1850. Hexthorpe station was built near the Greenfield Lane bridge and Sprotborough was won from nature by cutting a meagre recess into the rock side of the deep cutting and providing a ledge of approximately 12in width to serve as a platform. Access was by a flight of 66 steps, again cut into the rock face. The Midland Railway worked passenger services from Sheffield (Wicker) to Doncaster via Swinton and the Great Northern began working the freight traffic from 1 July 1851 when the line was finally completed to Barnsley. The coal traffic was an extremely lucrative business right from the start of the GN service, and the SYR built a short siding at Strawberry Island to give the trains good access to the barges on the Don.

The GNR Reaches Doncaster

The opening of the South Yorkshire line was originally intended to take place in time for the 1849 St Leger week, but last-minute problems with the Don bridge at Conisbrough ruled this out. Nevertheless, the race week was notable for the opening of another important piece of railway, the GNR's Retford-Doncaster section. This line connected the town with the GNR's main line from London to the north, albeit a rather long-winded one in 1849, and gave an alternative route to London to that provided by the NMR from Swinton. From Retford trains reached Lincoln via the MSLR route (as agreed in 1848), and then travelled via Boston, Spalding and Cambridge *en route* to Bishopgate Street station in London.

Great indeed was the commotion leading up to the public opening of the railway on Tuesday 4 September. The necessary inspection was carried out by Captain Lafan, accompanied by the resident engineer Henry Carr and the representative of the contractors, Peto & Betts, George Tate. Local press excitement pointed to the GNR being the salvation of the town, particularly as the coaching trade had virtually disappeared and parts of the Great North Road had actually *become overgrown* due to lack of use. The event was described as '. . . the re-opening of the Great Highway to the North by the application of science and skill through the instrumentality of steam and iron rails'.

Despite such feelings, no opening ceremony was held. Locomotives and rolling stock were delivered on the previous day and presented a colourful spectacle in the evening sunlight after their arrival at 18.00. Seven green locomotives built by Hawthorn's of Newcastle and an assortment of claret-coloured rolling stock were all parked ready for the start of public services. Crowds duly assembled at every possible viewpoint, and the first train set off at 08.30 amidst cheering and bell-ringing. The first arrival took place at 09.00, when a party from Retford de-trained for a breakfast at the Mansion House after a journey of 41 minutes duration. South of the town the new line passed through countryside which for generations had been disturbed by nothing more intrusive than horse-drawn farm carts. The Hexthorpe road was crossed on the level, close to the Union workhouse, and after the Cherry Lane Junction with the SYR the

Right:
The 08.55 Hull-Sheffield passes St James' Junction on 25 July 1971.
T. G. Flinders

Below:
Today's layout at Hexthorpe deals with express passenger workings and also with coal traffic at the mgr stabling yard. Class 47/8 No 47824 *Glorious Devon* passes by with the 09.21 Bristol-York on 30 April 1990.
S. R. Batty

Far right:
The GNR's southern exit from Doncaster cuts across meadow and pasture towards Retford. Here Class O4/8 No 63858 plods across Black Carr with a train of down empties on 24 August 1957. *R. E. Vincent*

line passed through the garden of a Mr Ellison, behind St James's cottage. (The SYR junction was referred to at the time as either Cherry Lane or Cherry Tree Lane.) A short brick tunnel was built below Balby Road by a Mr Moody, who had also constructed all the brickwork along the earlier line from Doncaster to Arksey. The bricks were produced from clay dug out of a large area adjacent to the line as it headed towards Bawtry and known locally as the City of Sods! The brickfields became disused after completion of the railway works and soon filled with water, giving some slight variation to the scenery of the vast and useless boggy area of Doncaster Carr. The line was carried on an unusual embankment which was 4-5ft high on one side only, with a canal-like waterway on the other (low) side. Many held hopes that efforts would soon be made to drain completely this large, marshy area and turn the land to better use. The new brickwork of the small bridges and drainage channels and the smart appearance of freshly-painted white fences and crossing gates were generally felt to have smartened up the countryside a

great deal, and complemented the rural beauty of St Catherine's church and well, Wadworth Wood and Edlington Wood. Decoy plantation was bisected by the line, and was described as '. . . lately noted for families of lizards, snakes and other reptiles, as well as birds of prey, secure in their almost undisturbed abodes, with wild raspberry trees and specimens of flowers of rare descriptions'.

Thus the line continued on to Retford, carving across the Arcadian rurality of South Yorkshire and North Nottinghamshire and bringing the GNR almost within direct reach of York. However, George Hudson's Knottingley-Burton Salmon connection was not ready due to problems with Stephenson's tubular bridge crossing of the river Aire at Brotherton. One tube was brought into use by April 1850, but it was not until October 1852 that the work was finally completed. (The bridge is still in use today, carrying a large amount of heavy freight traffic, although the tubular construction was replaced by a lattice girder arrangement during the early years of the present century.) The 1849 St Leger was held less than two

weeks after the opening, and more than 10,000 passengers used the new GNR service. The Manchester, Sheffield & Lincolnshire Railway ran trains to the town via Retford and the LYR ran specials from Wakefield, Bradford, Huddersfield, Halifax and Manchester. Trains arrived from Leeds, York, Harrogate, Ripon and Newcastle, and the North Midland service from Sheffield and Rotherham to Swinton ensured heavy road and river traffic from here to Doncaster. The traffic flowed smoothly, and the excellent arrangements reflected great credit on the stationmaster of the time, Mr Chadwick.

Left:
Class A3 4-6-2 No 60106 *Flying Fox* arrives from King's Cross on a freezing 27 February 1955. *G. Warnes*

Below left:
Doncaster's Bridge Junction controlled access between the GNR and SYR lines south of the station. This is Class 47/4 No 47458 snaking across to the up fast line with a King's Cross express on 14 August 1975. St James' Bridge station and Garden sidings can be seen on the left, and Shakespeare dock on the right. *L. A. Nixon*

Below:
The approach frcm the south today - Class 91 No 91002 passes below Balby Rd with the 12.10 King's Cross-Leeds on 18 September 1990. *S. R. Batty*

During October 1849 the GNR took over the running of the Knottingley passenger service from the LYR and also exercised its running powers over the former North Midland route from Methley to Leeds. The GNR's access from London to the north was nearing completion, but work on the last vital stretch from Peterborough to Retford did not start until late 1849 and progress was delayed by the tunnel works at Stoke and Peascliffe. Originally scheduled for opening in late 1851, goods services did not start until 15 July 1852 and passenger services until 1 August. The King's Cross-York-Leeds journey was shortened by 20 miles and journey times reduced to 6.5 hours and 6 hours respectively, times which could not be bettered by the rival Midland Railway. Progress had been achieved at an amazing rate — in 1846 the company received its Act after a Parliamentary battle of staggering proportions which consumed vast amounts of time, effort and money, yet by 1852 it had built almost 200 miles of railway which· was engineered for speed and capacity to equal any other in the Kingdom. Denison's comment of 1847 regarding the 'ploughed field' terminus at Askern Junction pointed to a situation which simply could not be tolerated if the company was to expand beyond Doncaster. Direct routes to Leeds and York, independent of any other company, were needed urgently but were not to be built until the GNR had sufficient capital available for such large works.

Right:
St James' Junction, 1977.
J. H. Turner

Below:
The 08.15 Newcastle-Penzance accelerates past today's mgr sidings on 28 July 1990. Coal traffic has been handled at Hexthorpe for almost 150 years. *S. R. Batty*

Far right:
Class 56 No 56079 eases a well-filled mgr train into Hexthorpe Yard on 30 April 1990. *S. R. Batty*

Expansion of the South Yorkshire Railway

The early working arrangements between the South Yorkshire and Great Northern Railways worked well for some five years until railway politics soured relations somewhat. The GN-worked coal traffic from the Barnsley coalfield resulted in over 20 trains per day being sent southwards from Doncaster, and the Midland-worked passenger service from Sheffield was using the SYR Cherry Lane station. But during 1849

the notorious 'Euston Square Confederacy' was formed between the Midland, the Manchester, Sheffield & Lincolnshire, the Lancashire & Yorkshire and the London & North Western Railways, with the clear intention of starving the infant GNR of traffic. This was principally an LNWR plan which had the MSLR involved rather, one suspects, against its better judgement, whereas the Midland Railway saw the exercise as an extension of Hudson's anti-GNR feeling. Although being heavily involved with the GNR, the South Yorkshire nevertheless worked from the

heart of Midland territory, crossing its main line at Swinton, and could easily have fallen into MR hands. (A connecting curve between the SYR and MR is believed to have been authorised during 1847 and opened in 1850.) Although the SYR had offices at the GNR station in Doncaster, the MR-worked passenger trains were confined to the SYR station until 1852.

Thus the GNR and MR were firmly at odds with each other, and the SYR was caught in the middle. The GNR was making a good profit from the SYR coal traffic and was not prepared to see the little company snatched out of its hand by any rival, and certainly not by the MR. Leasing arrangements were sought by the MSLR, the MR and the GNR, and the latter was successful in obtaining the necessary Act in June 1852. Strings, however, were attached. The Midland successfully petitioned Parliament to allow a curve to be built at Swinton to allow SYR traffic to be taken via its main line if required and so prevent a total GNR monopoly. (Sources vary as to whether the original curve of 1847-50 was ever built, but this 1852 proposal — the Adwick curve — certainly put a Midland cat among GN pigeons!) Talks between the GNR and SYR during October 1851 had led to an agreement whereby the GNR would lease the SYR for a period of 21 years before finally taking over the company in its entirety, but this mutually acceptable arrangement was scuppered by the GNR when the Midland was granted the right to build the Adwick curve. From this point onwards the good GNR/SYR relationship deteriorated into disputes and legal actions, resulting in the GNR deciding to do nothing about the proposed amalgamation. At the end of 1854 the matter was closed formally when all accounts were settled and all agreements became void. The SYR was free of any leasing (or amalgamation) threat for the time being, but had quickly to obtain some motive power to replace that which had been withdrawn by the GNR. Eventually the coal trains began

running into Hexthorpe yard under SYR power, but the GNR had gained nothing from the exercise.

The South Yorkshire Company's Act had laid down that amalgamation with the Dun Navigation Co should take place when half the railway company's capital had been raised and spent, and this was accomplished by April 1850. Consequently, when the SYR decided to build its railway onwards from Doncaster to reach the Humber, the company already owned sufficient land to build a railway (of sorts) without having to go to the expense of obtaining an Act of Parliament. Thorne could be reached by building a line alongside the Don navigation, and the Stainforth & Keadby canal, which the company also owned, from Strawberry Island at Doncaster to Thorne Waterside. The single line was a succession of extremely tight curves which were heavily restricted for speed and ran perilously close the the canal. One locomotive at least is known to have ended up at the bottom of the Navigation, but it appears that the SYR was quite happy to accept such inconveniences for the sake of better coal-unloading facilities at Waterside.

Coal traffic commenced running on Tuesday 11 December 1855 when, at 12 noon, a train of 10 wagons was unloaded into barges which promptly set sail for Hull. Some celebration of the opening took place at Thorne, and the first train was decorated with flags and bunting in the usual style of such events. Temperance, not a usual part in these events, was celebrated by a band of teetotal workmen who placed their own banners on the locomotive, only to have them promptly removed by the more dissolute members of the workforce! Passenger services ran to Thorne Lock from July 1856 and called at the intermediate stations of Barnby Dun, Bramwith and Stainforth. A passenger boat service connected at Thorne and sailed on to Keadby and Hull, but the end result was that travellers from Doncaster were faced with a

Above:
The SYR station at Thorne, looking towards Scunthorpe at about the turn of the century. *P. Cookson collection*

Right:
The SYR's Thorne station today, with a Sprinter DMU departing on a Sheffield-Cleethorpes train on 16 July 1990. *S. R. Batty*

journey along a ramshackle mineral railway before being subjected to the uncertainties of a treacherous river passage down the Humber. Such a state of affairs belonged to the 1830s and could not be tolerated for long. In 1858 the SYR started work on extending the line from Thorne eastwards to Keadby, once again using the canal bank as a roadway and avoiding the need for an Act of Parliament or any other great expense. Opening took place in September 1859 and the only intermediate station was at Crowle, with Maud's Bridge, Medge Hall and Godnow Bridge being built soon afterwards. A new station was built at Thorne, on the new Keadby line, and the original station at Thorne Lock was closed after just over three years of use.

Peace Again

After the upsets caused by the Euston Square Confederacy of the early 1850s had been overcome, the SYR and the GNR once again settled down to jointly handling the coal traffic from Barnsley to the coast and southwards to London. Over the years from 1852 to 1867 an annual tonnage of approximately 3.3 million tons was taken by sea from the Barnsley coalfield to London. Whereas this figure remained almost unchanged over the 15-year period, the rail-borne tonnage increased from 378,000 in 1852 (i.e. before

the GNR was in business) to 1,138,000 tons in 1855 and to well over 3 million tons by 1867. This rising tide of profit ensured that the GNR and SYR worked to each other's mutual advantage, but it also attracted the attention of some powerful neighbours in the forms of the Lancashire & Yorkshire Railway, North Eastern Railway and even the distant Great Eastern Railway. By 1860 the town's prosperity was set for a long association with the coal-mining business, at first through the transportation of Barnsley coal and later through the development of the Doncaster coalfield. This latter event lay some 35 years into the future, but the 1860s were to see the town's railway connections expanded almost to their final form.

Above right:
A packed scene at Stainforth & Hatfield in April 1961, as Class O2/3 No 63969 heads westwards with a steel train and two trainloads head towards Scunthorpe past Hatfield colliery. The yards to the south of the lines are well filled, and a Class 08 shunter is busy on the north side. *J. C. Baker*

Right:
A view from almost the same position as in the previous photograph, but taken nearly 30 years later. Class 47 No 47221 heads an up Speedlink service through the station on 2 March 1990. *S. R. Batty*

3: Developments of the 1860s

The West Riding & Grimsby Railway

The simplest way for the GNR and SYR to improve their coal business was to build a new railway direct from Thorne via Goole to Hull, where the docks could handle trade for London and also for export to continental Europe. Only one very large problem presented itself here, the single fact that Hull was in the heart of North Eastern Railway territory where no opposition to the NER coal trade monopoly was to be countenanced. Nevertheless, a GNR/SYR proposal was made in 1861 and the NER quickly made some appeasing moves towards the GNR before the scheme went to Parliament in 1862. The Bill was rejected, but the opening shot had been fired in a series of manoeuvres aimed at capturing the haulage of long-distance coal traffic from Doncaster.

Subsequently the mid-1860s saw a confusing series of moves being made by all the companies involved. In 1863 the NER and SYR came to an agreement for a new route to Hull; the NER would build from Staddlethorpe Junction (on the Hull-Selby line) down to Thorne, and the SYR would rebuild its own line (the canal-bank mineral line) from here into Doncaster. Running powers would be granted whereby the NER would work into Doncaster and the GNR would reach Hull. The scheme was passed by Parliament in July of that year, but six years were to pass before the NER built the new line. The swing bridge at Goole and a stock market crash in May 1867 both delayed the opening from the original date of May 1868 to August 1869, when the distance from Doncaster to Hull was shortened to 40 miles. Also during 1863 the SYR was

Below:
The West Riding & Grimsby line from Adwick Junction to Stainforth crossed the Don by a swing bridge, seen here in the 'open' position during the early 1950s. *C. T. Goode*

leased by the Manchester, Sheffield & Lincolnshire Railway, and the new owners wasted no time in improving the full ex-SYR system from end to end. The Keadby line, far from being abandoned after the NER/SYR agreement, was improved radically by the MSLR to serve the new Scunthorpe ironworks which was built from 1864. The Kirk Sandall-Maud's Bridge section was re-opened after rebuilding during November 1866 and the section from Doncaster to Kirk Sandall was completed during the following month. Powers for improving the rest of the line to Keadby were obtained during the same year, and plans for doubling the line all the way to Grimsby were being made.

This period also saw the beginning of the end of the GNR's dependence on the LYR and MR for access to Leeds and York. During the 1850s the GNR had promoted two West Riding railway companies, the Bradford, Wakefield & Leeds Railway and the Leeds, Bradford & Halifax Junction Railway, both of which it had absorbed and so gained a very strong foothold in the industrial heartland of the Leeds/Bradford area. Several attempts had been made by the GNR to build its own railway direct from Doncaster to Wakefield and so connect these systems with the main line, but all had failed. The LYR was the GNR's principal foe in the West Riding, and independent access *had* to be built to ensure the future of the empire. In one of its last acts before amalgamation with the MSLR, the South Yorkshire provided the GNR with an almost tailor-made solution to their West Riding problem. Even before agreement with the NER over the Doncaster-Thorne-Staddlethorpe line, the SYR was planning to build from Wakefield south-eastwards to Stainforth to provide a direct link between the West Riding and Hull via the SYR's original Thorne-Hull line, and a branch from Adwick was to reach directly into Doncaster via a junction with the GNR main line just north of the station. Known initially as the West Riding, Hull & Grimsby Railway, the scheme was intended to reach Hull by the SYR-proposed new route to Hull and to reach Grimsby by the proposed extension onwards from Keadby. Amazingly, the railway was authorised by Parliament in 1862 in the face of opposition from the NER and LYR, which already controlled access into Hull, and one imagines the GNR was totally dismayed at the ease with which the company had gained approval for a line to Wakefield. After the SYR/NER agreement in 1863 the Hull extension was dropped from the plans and the railway became known as the West Riding & Grimsby. Problems, however, prevented the GNR from making a straightforward take-over of the WRGR. The Great

Above:
This enthusiasts' special of the mid-1960s saw Class O4/1 No 63585 hauling a rare passenger working between Skellow Junction, on the Leeds-Stainforth line, and Carcroft Junction on the Doncaster-Leeds leg of the WRGR. The train is seen here at Carcroft Junction. *P. Cookson*

Right:
A Leeds-Cleethorpes excursion passes Bramwith malt kilns on the WRGR, behind Class B1 4-6-0 No 61268. The somersault signal is pure GNR, and the train is made up of two Gresley King's Cross 'Quad-Art' sets. *G. Warnes*

Eastern Railway was formed in 1862, late in terms of railway development, and found itself heavily dependent on a web of lines spread across East Anglia and the Fens, carrying very little apart from agricultural traffic. Passenger traffic from London was healthy enough, but a regular, profitable goods traffic was needed, and the GER's eyes fell (like many others) on the Doncaster-London coal trade. With this end in mind the GER promoted the March & Askern Coal Railway in 1862, to build a new railway to meet the LYR and so give this latter company an opportunity to expand southwards. The GNR naturally opposed this and the scheme was lost, but the GER did not give up and the GNR also found itself threatened by LYR plans to drive a new line around Doncaster. The Great Eastern's trunk route proposal found support from the ever-ambitious South Yorkshire and also from the MSLR, who already operated well towards GER territory and would relish some further expansion by virtue of running powers. And herein lay the crux of the problem — the SYR/MSLR amalgamation of 1863 *could* have seen the GER gain a clear path to the West Riding via the SYR-backed WRGR scheme which had been approved in 1862. By this time the GNR was a past master at buying out smaller railway companies, but now it would have to do business with the MSLR. This was not a bad thing from either point of view as the two companies had — apart from some sulking during the years of the Confederacy — always got on well together. Before any agreements were made, however, the GER attacked again with requests for running powers over existing lines towards Askern, and the GN revived its plans of 1847/48 for building a direct Doncaster-Gainsborough line. These moves smacked of more than a little desperation on behalf of both companies in their efforts to out-do each other, and were thrown out of Parliament in the 1863 session. Railway politicking then took a hand and during 1864 the GN's Gainsborough line was approved, together with yet another proposal being made for a new railway from Cambridge to the WRGR at Adwick. The LYR was again involved, but the coal railway proposal was finally buried during 1865, leaving the GNR with a new line

to be built to Gainsborough and also free to negotiate with the MSLR over the future of the West Riding & Grimsby. With the GER's plans for a new line now disposed of, the MSLR no longer faced a conflict of interest between its desire on the one hand to expand into the eastern counties, and on the other to run the new Wakefield line jointly with the GNR. A leasing arrangement was made in 1866, the year of the WRGR opening, which gave the MSLR access to Wakefield and onwards to Leeds Central, and which also allowed the GNR to work through to Grimsby.

On Thursday 1 February 1886 the GNR's independent access to Leeds and Bradford became a reality with the opening of the Doncaster-Adwick-Wakefield line. Mr Francis F. Cockshott, the Assistant Manager of the GNR, was present to witness the departure of the first train to Wakefield at 09.17, calling at all stations except the incomplete buildings at Adwick-le-Street. Ten trains daily operated in each direction,

with three on Sundays, but the GN at first did not promote the new line and did not even bother to publish a timetable, causing many to wonder if the company was really interested in local passenger services. The section from Adwick Junction to Stainforth opened in November of the same year, when the SYR's Doncaster-Thorne improvements were completed, but bad weather caused flooding problems between Tilts and Owston which caused the line to be closed during the same month. A through passenger service to Grimsby from Leeds was postponed from its intended opening date of 1 December, and goods traffic did not start using the line until 5 July 1867. A goods depot only was provided on the Adwick-Stainforth line at Barnby Dun, renamed Bramwith in February 1882, but passenger stations were ready for the opening at South Elmsall, Hemsworth, Nostell, and at Sandall, with the station at Adwick being completed during the following month. The station here was renamed Carcroft & Adwick-le-Street in May 1880, and a further station was opened along the line at Hare Park & Crofton in November 1885.

By the mid-1860s the GNR and MSLR had created a railway system through Doncaster which gave both companies access to the West Riding area, with its enormous traffic potential, and to the future steelworks and ports along the south bank of the Humber and the north Lincolnshire coastline.

Joint Line Construction: The GN/GE Joint Line

After the failure of the GER's trunk route proposals in 1865, the company resorted to other tactics to try and gain a foothold in Doncaster. Running powers, joint building of new lines in the Fens and even amalgamation between the GER and GNR, were all discussed at various times, but the only agreement reached was for the joint building of a line from Spalding to March with mutual exchange of running powers. Meanwhile the GNR went ahead with building the Gainsborough line, a relatively easy piece of railway running from a junction off the GNR at Potteric Carr for a distance of 18 miles with a maximum gradient of 1 in 400. Stations were built at Finning-

Below:
The Adwick-Stainforth section of the WRGR includes a steep climb from Shaftholme to allow the ECML to be crossed. Class 56 No 56089 labours up the grade with a load of coal for Thorpe Marsh power station on 16 May 1990. *S. R. Batty*

Right:
The station buildings survive today at Carcroft & Adwick-le-Street, only a few misplaced slates and a satellite dish spoiling the general appearance. A Class 307 EMU passes through on a crew-training run on 16 May 1990. *S. R. Batty*

ley, Haxey for Epworth, Misterton, Walkeringham and at Beckingham, but the expected opening date of spring 1866 was not attained and the line did not open until 1 July 1867 for goods traffic, passengers following on 15 July. By this time the Spalding-March line had opened, and traffic — particularly goods and coal — was soon running from Doncaster via Retford (and the MSLR) to Lincoln, thence to Boston and Spalding (via the old GN main line) and on to March and the GER. Eventually, in 1879, after yet more argument over GER/GNR matters, the two companies set up a Great Northern/Great Eastern Joint Committee which took control of the Gainsborough line and the Spalding-March line and also

gained powers to build the missing links in a system which would finally reach beyond March to St Ives and Godmanchester, near Huntingdon. Several existing lines were taken over by the Joint Committee at the southern end of the system and the lines from Gainsborough to Lincoln and Lincoln to Spalding were completed during 1882. The GER had finally reached Doncaster and the GNR reached well into the 'Swedey's' territory by a joint line.

Four trains each way daily commenced operating from 15 July 1867, but a Plant works trip of 6 July was the first passenger train to use the line en route to Grimsby and Cleethorpes via Gainsborough and Barnetby. No less than 4,000 free passes were issued for travel on the four trains due to depart between 06.00 and 07.00, and the station area was besieged by swarming, heaving masses of people, many of whom had turned up just to watch the spectacle. The Plant Volunteer Band went along too, and the works committee, which had organised the trip, travelled in first class rolling stock. It was a gloriously hot and sunny day, and as the trains crossed the baked countryside the correspondent of the *Doncaster Gazette* painted a word picture of luxuriant hedges, ripening corn, scarlet poppies, silver dykes and tumbling haystacks. He also made a comment on the labourers in the fields who saw the amazing procession, referring to '...astonished rustics leaning on their hay forks...' — which implies that Doncaster still had a strong rural element to everyday life, even in the 1860s. A water stop was made at Gainsborough, and Grimsby was

Left:
'Deltic' No 55008 approaches Black Carr Junction with a down express in October 1977. The GN/GE Joint line can be seen to the left, passing below the later Dearne Valley line.
P. C. H. Robinson

Below left:
Class 47/4 No. 47592 *County of Avon* clears Bessacarr Junction and heads towards Gainsborough with a late-running 10.37 Leeds-Skegness on 1 September 1990.
S. R. Batty

Below:
The 11.19 Sleaford-Doncaster ambles through the countryside near Park Drain on 16 July 1990. *S. R. Batty*

Top left:
Class O4/8 2-8-0 No 63818 approaches Doncaster North Junction with an up goods on 11 July 1964. The Leeds lines can be seen in the foreground. *A. W. Martin*

Above left:
Also on 11 July 1964, one of Doncaster's Standard Class 9F 2-10-0 allocation, No 92174, passes below the GCR avoiding line with an up petrol train near Doncaster North Junction. *A. W. Martin*

Left:
Class B1 4-6-0 No 61272 makes a vigorous start out of the station with the 10.45(SO) Skegness-York on 15 August 1964. On the left, Class K1 2-6-0 No 62014 can be seen arriving with an up goods train. *J. S. Hancock*

Above:
A train of empty flat wagons passes below the North Bridge behind Class 40 No 40081 on 4 July 1975. *J. E. Oxley*

reached in 2hr 30min from Doncaster via MSLR metals, the latter town being a busy fishing port on the verge of industrial expansion, but nearby Cleethorpes was described merely as a 'stagnating village'. The return trains covered the 22 miles from Gainsborough in 30 minutes, at 'express speed', and the last arrival took place at 23.00.

The East Coast Main Line

The Hudson route from Doncaster to York via Knottingley and Church Fenton was a rather rambling way of connecting two such important railway centres, and in 1864 the North Eastern Railway obtained powers by an Act of 23 March to build a new line from Chaloner Whin Junction, south of York, to pass through Selby (using the Leeds-Selby-Hull line from Barlby junction to Canal Junction) and meet the GNR at Shaftholme junction, near Owston. Apart from some curvature at Selby, this line was virtually straight and level and was free of junctions along almost all its length. A swing bridge was built across the Ouse at Naburn, south of York, and this caused some delay with the final opening which eventually took place, six months late, on 2 January 1871. No ceremony took place, but the King's Cross-York journey time was reduced to 5hr and the express traffic disappeared from the Knottingley route. Running powers allowed the GN to work into York, and the company had at last freed itself of any ties to the LYR for access to York and the north. The new railway had been built by Thomas Nelson of Carlisle for a cost of £239,500. A goods-only connection was laid in during 1877 from Joan Croft Junction, immediately north of Shaftholme Junction, to Applehurst junction on the WRGR Adwick-Stainforth line.

4: The Plant

The Early Years

As mentioned earlier, the town of Doncaster suffered a rapid decline in trade after the opening of the North Midland Railway in 1840. Although the coming of the railways from 1848 to 1852 gave a boost to the flagging local economy, what was really needed was the presence of a large employer which would finance the future development of the town.

The Great Northern began looking for a suitable site for a locomotive repair works almost as soon as the company was incorporated, and, at first, established a small works at Boston, on the Fens line, to the south. As early as 1846, Doncaster corporation set out to entice the company into the town to build the bigger works which the GNR quickly realised it would need. On 24 August a public meeting was held to determine a course of action, and 200 signatures were placed on a petition which was then sent to the GNR. Edmund Denison, his son Edmund Beckett Denison, and Robert Baxter of the lawyers Baxter, Rose & Norton set about the task of persuading the GNR board to put its new works in the town. It was not an easy task, as many directors and officers of the company initially favoured the alternative sites offered at Peterborough and Retford. William Cubitt, the GNR's first locomotive engineer, favoured Peterborough due to its 'central location' on the GNR system. His early death saw the post filled by Edward Bury, of the locomotive builders Bury, Curtis & Kennedy, but he was too busy building locomotives for other railways to be of much use to the GNR, and in April 1850 he was replaced by the 34-year-old Archibald Sturrock from the Great Western Railway. Sturrock also favoured Peterborough. On the other hand many directors favoured using land at Retford which had already been staked out.

Denison continued his campaign. During 1847, negotiations had been started for a large amount of land — the 'station ground' — to be bought for the GNR's use. A committee was formed to look into the relative merits of all the sites and make recommendations to the board, and in June 1851 the decision was taken to build at Doncaster. The main points in the town's favour were good water communications and plentiful nearby supplies of coal and iron. Baxter and Denison must have certainly used all their industrial connections in the face of strong opposition from virtually all the rest of the GN board, and indeed from some in the town itself who feared the results of such

an industrial invasion. The decision was announced to great rejoicing, and the negotiations for land purchase were completed during 1852. The agreed purchase money had already been paid to the Lords of the Treasury, and in April 1852 this was transferred to the town corporation, as Lords of the Manor, for distribution to the benefit of the Common Right owners. The freemen of Doncaster were compensated for the loss of their grazing rights in Crimpsall meadow, and the freeholds of various houses in Hexthorpe and Balby were also bought. Some doubters remained apprehensive about the possible effects of such a change to the character of the town, but the *Doncaster Gazette* was in no doubt at all about where the future lay. On 10 October 1851 an editorial feature stated:

'This gigantic scheme is well calculated to give a stimulus to the trade of the town and will add materially to increase its population. We look upon the Plant as the pioneer of future prosperity to the inhabitants and we trust that, by the great facilities afforded by the railway operations, Doncaster is yet destined to enjoy the return of that prosperity which it experienced in the good old days of posting and coaching.'

The GNR lost no time in getting the work started, and on 3 March 1852 tenders were invited for building the new works. Just how quickly the GNR moved — and it expected contractors to be equally as brisk — can be judged from the fact that the tenders had to be handed into King's Cross in time for a board meeting on 23 March, less than three weeks after being invited. A large number was submitted, however, and the contract was awarded to the firm of G. & H. Holme from Liverpool, which estimated the cost at £80,000. This may not have been the cheapest quotation, but Holme himself had worked with Brassey, one of the great railway building contractors, on the construction of the GNR main line, and the board may have already been well-pleased with his company's earlier work. The contract was for the erection of the company's *repairing* shops; no mention was made of any intention to *build* locomotives or rolling stock at this time, and several years were to pass before any work of this type was to be undertaken. Holme also tendered successfully for building a new public roadway above the SYR/GNR tracks to the south of the station. Three level crossings had previously been constructed in the town, at Marsh Gate on the Great North Road, at the north-west end of West Laithe Gate near the junction with Hexthorpe Lane, and at Cherry Lane. Parliamentary approval was given for stopping the right of way over the GNR line at the last two places and for the building of the new bridge. For the bridge, Holme proposed a brick structure with stone abutments using seven arches over a length of 300yd supporting a 30ft roadway. In the event he used Mexborough stone, cut from new quarries and taken to the site by water transport and horse and cart. The bridge was described as 'a convenient approach to the public walks and pleasure grounds of Hexthorpe Flatts — when they are built.' Work started on the Plant in May 1852 and was to be finished within 12 months. One casualty was St James' Barn, the last remains of a 13th century leper hospital, which was totally destroyed.

In 1851, Balby with Hexthorpe consisted of 23 houses occupied by professional people or farmers, all of whom had servants. The area was earmarked for housing development, and by early 1852 speculative builders had gained consent to erect 300 houses off St James Street, to be used by the men expected to transfer from the Boston works during 1853. By the summer of that year, half of the 700 men from Lincolnshire had arrived in the town to find 120 cottages ready and no less than a further 300 being built. Most of the jobs were taken by the Boston men, but some were filled by local labour and the general effect on the town's prosperity was to improve matters to a level hardly imaginable just a few years before.

Other improvements followed, due entirely to Denison's philanthropic nature and his strength on the GNR board. He was fully aware of the problems which could have been caused by building a large works in a small town and transferring large numbers of men and their families over a considerable distance to unfamiliar surroundings. He was concerned for the welfare of the workforce, and proposed that the GNR should build a church and a school at a cost of approximately £8,000. He stated, quite straightforwardly, that 'I will not be a party to bringing some 3,000 souls into the town without making some provision for their spiritual welfare'. His proposals were discussed at a shareholders' meeting in February 1854, and attracted much opposition. One shareholder wondered if the GNR was intended to be a railway company or a church extension society. For once, Denison did not get his own way and had to rely on the directors digging into their own pockets to fund the building of the church, through endowments and subscriptions. St James' Church finally consecrated on 15 October 1857, after costing £11,000 during building. Perhaps the shareholders thought Denison had done enough towards making life a little more bearable for the GNR employees, at least as far as *their* capital was concerned. A sickness society had been formed in 1850, (St James' hospital was opened in 1852 funded by the local gentry), a reading room was opened in 1853 and a library was due to open in 1854, together with a Mechanics Institute. Throughout the country generally, industrial conditions were at their worst, and employment in the foundry, railway and engineering trades was a grim affair where hardship was commonplace and injury or death was a regular happening. Enlightened employers were few and far between in the 1850s. Doncaster's new hospital, supervised by Dr Dunn, was certainly needed — the railways had brought many accidents, and the town had a total lack of any alternative facilities.

The Plant's First Engine

The Plant came into use during the summer of 1853 as each of the shops was completed. During June, a 40hp stationary steam engine was successfully started at the first attempt by the manufacturers, Jones & Carmichael of Dundee; Archibald Sturrock must have held great misgivings about the ability of this engine to even turn a wheel under its own power, for he gave a supper to the workmen involved as a mark of his gratitude and astonishment! With machine power available, the shops were quickly put to use and the builders then moved on to the next area of construction. The first set of GNR men to arrive at the new works was a group of smiths under a Mr David Denham, and by the year-end a total of 950 were employed on the site. As built, a total of 11 acres were enclosed and five acres were under cover, but expansion of the initial facilities started almost immediately, the smithy being enlarged in 1854.

Briefly, the Plant consisted of a long block parallel to and facing the down main line, with five further blocks built behind this and separated by various roadways. The long block contained turning shops, a grinding shop, a carriage shop, a boiler house and engine room, stores, workmen's baths and offices for the locomotive engineer, works manager, the timekeeper and the draughtsmen. Of the separate blocks built behind the offices the most southerly held a boiler shop, a coppersmiths shop and a brass foundry, the latter having four crucible hearths and the boiler shop having an overhead traveller for moving boilers as required. The erecting shop was the heart of the Plant, where up to 30 locomotives could be repaired at any one time on the 15 pits either side of the centre bay. A large smithy was built with 15 single hearths and 19 double ones, where blooms could be heated before being worked on with steam hammers, but, as mentioned earlier, this capacity proved inadequate and the smithy was soon enlarged. (No foundry existed at this time, and all castings were bought into the Plant from outside suppliers.) An adjacent wagon shop had 19 roads and areas for drying and storing timber, and the adjoining carriage

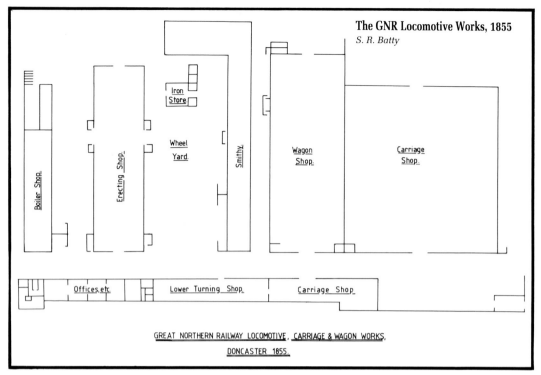

The GNR Locomotive Works, 1855
S. R. Batty

Boiler Shop.

Erecting Shop.

Iron
Store

Wheel
Yard.

Smithy

Wagon
Shop.

Carriage
Shop.

Offices,etc.   Lower Turning Shop.   Carriage Shop.

GREAT NORTHERN RAILWAY LOCOMOTIVE, CARRIAGE & WAGON WORKS,

DONCASTER 1855.

Right:
**Stirling 8ft single No 8 was built in December 1870 as works
No 61.** *NRM (LBSC 93)*

Above right:
**These carriage connections, between a pair of six-wheelers,
were typical before the use of side chains was discontinued
from 1904. The vehicles are piped for vacuum and
Westinghouse brakes, and the buffers are of convex~concave
pattern.** *NRM (Don 366)*

shop was of similar layout although it had only 16
roads. A collection of smaller buildings housed coke
ovens, manual fire engines and an iron store.

Locomotives of the period were all supplied by
contractors to the designs of the GNR locomotive
superintendent. Principal suppliers were R. W.
Hawthorne, R. Stephenson, Kitsons, and Sharpe,
Stewart. Hawthorne built the first locomotive to Sturrock's instructions in 1853, when 4-2-2 No 215 was
produced. Sturrock liked to see plenty of firebox
heating area and a high boiler pressure, and No. 215's
150lb/sq in boiler gave plenty of steam to turn the 7ft
6in driving wheels. Unfortunately, she was prone to
derailing, but lasted in service until 1869.

The idea of using a smaller steam engine to boost
locomotive power by driving trailing wheels or tender wheels cropped up at various times in
GNR/LNER history, but Sturrock can claim to have
been first with the idea in the early 1860s when he
designed a steam tender for use with a class of small-

boilered 5ft 0in 0-6-0 goods locos. The idea worked well up to a point, as the locomotives so fitted could haul trains which were too long to be handled comfortably on the running lines, but despite having condensers fitted inside the tenders, steam gushed everywhere and made life very difficult for the crew. Although 70 were ordered, delivery was stopped and the existing equipment removed.

Enlargements to the Plant continued, possibly with a view to building locomotives as soon as facilities would allow. An interesting development was the provision of the Plant's own gas generation and supply system which was fully in use by 1866. The 1864 gas bill had totalled no less than £1,200, and gas engineers Knapton & Co were engaged to supply retorts and gas holders to supply the Plant's 6,000 lights. The main contract (for the 35 retorts and two 60ft x 20ft gasholders) was awarded to Anelay's, but the modifications to the gas mains necessary to remove the system from the public supply were carried out by W. S. Smith & Son of Baxter Gate. During 1865 plans were made to enlarge the erecting shop and a new steam hammer shop measuring 45ft x 157ft was built in Crimpsall yard at a cost of £50,000. Raw materials were brought in from far and wide, and in

May 1866 Sturrock stated (to a Royal Commission on railways) that he was '...using Krupps steel from Germany, Vickers and Butchers steel from Sheffield, and Monkbridge, Taylor Brothers and Bowlings steel from Leeds'.

During the same year, Sturrock was replaced as Locomotive Engineer by Patrick Stirling, and it was at the start of his long term of office that the 'official' decision was made to start building locomotives and rolling stock at the Plant. Stirling came to Doncaster as Works Manager (probably on the understanding that Sturrock's job would pass directly to him in due course) after serving 13 years as Locomotive Superintendent of the Glasgow & South Western Railway. Having being apprenticed to an uncle in Dundee, he worked for the Glasgow marine engineering company of Napier's as a fitter, before moving on to the locomotive department of Neilson & Co as a foreman. Various jobs followed, including that of Works Manager of R. W. Hawthorne & Co in Newcastle, before he moved to the GSWR in 1853 where he first made a name for himself in railway operating circles. Aged only 46 when appointed by the GNR, his 6ft 4in frame and distinguished manner left no-one in any doubt that a new broom had arrived to start a period

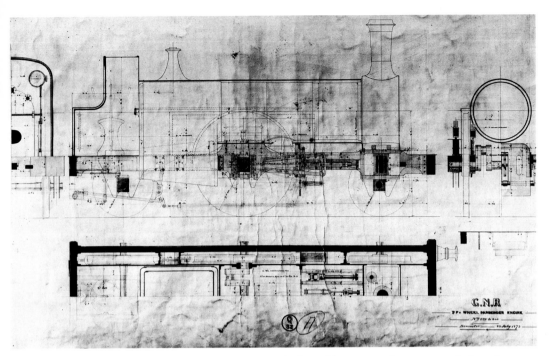

Left:
A two-horse omnibus for use around King's Cross station, built at the Plant in 1898. *NRM (Don A32)*

Above:
Part of a plan for Sturrock 2-2-2 locomotives Nos 229-40, dated July 1873. *NRM (Don 36/13)*

of locomotive design and construction work which would keep Doncaster at the top for many years to come. By 1895 he had produced no less than 899 locomotives for the GNR, 709 of which were constructed at the Plant.

Even though the works was being continually enlarged and improved, periods often came when locomotives had to be built by outside contractors simply because Doncaster was working at full capacity on construction and repair work. Stirling's appointment came at a particularly hectic period of works expansion. The erecting shop was extended in 1866 by a further 12 pits covering an area of 90ft x 104ft and giving a total area of 320ft x 102ft, which could hold 42 locomotives at any one time. A new section of the boiler shop was added to the south end of the existing one, and the alleyway between this and the erecting shop was roofed over to form a tender shop, complete with 35-ton hand cranes and equipment for slotting and drilling of locomotive and tender frames. The smithy was improved by the addition of a further four steam hammers and two bolt-forging machines, and the forge was equipped with a

further three steam hammers and four furnaces. (Waste heat from the furnaces was used to power the steam hammers.) A spring shop was built next to the smithy, covering only 120sq ft but using two furnaces and 12 hearths, and a larger brass foundry was built, also using 12 hearths, near the old western boundary of the works. Despite the tremendous capacity for metal-bashing, it was not until 1881 that a foundry was built for the production of cast iron. The three-bay building was fitted with an overhead crane and a small steam engine which powered the Roots blower to supply the draught to the single cupola. Perhaps the last significant alteration of the 1860s was the extension of the original north-south office block/turnery/carriage shop building at the north end, which allowed expansion of the machine shops and carriage works to the point where approximately 130 carriages could be built or repaired per year.

Stirling's first locomotive from the Plant was 0-4-2 No 18, which appeared in 1867. Three years later came the first of his 4-2-2 'Singles', the first locos to become famous as high-speed flyers of the East Coast main line. The 11ft 5in long boilers carried 217 brass tubes and were fitted with a copper 'mid-feather' across the firebox to increase water capacity and heating surface. A total of 37 were built up to 1882 and several modifications were made, perhaps the most successful being the rebuilding of two locos in 1884 with larger boilers, a smaller number of tubes and an increase in working pressure from 140lb/sq in to 160lb/sq in. To reflect the ever-increasing demands of the traffic department the tenders were enlarged over the years from 3.5 tons coal/2,700 gallons water

capacity to 5 tons/2,900 gallons. A last batch was built as late as 1895, somewhat modified from the original design with a boiler pressure of 170lb/sq in, 19.5in x 28in cylinders (the original size was 18in x 28in), brick-arch fireboxes and 5 tons/3,850 gallon tenders. The races to Aberdeen of 1895 were the 'Singles' finest hour; No 668 ran from King's Cross to Grantham, a distance of 105.5 miles, in 101 minutes, and after a *three-minute* engine change No 775 ran the 82.75 miles to York in 77 minutes, all with a 'flying' load of six coaches. Not bad for a 25-year-old design!

Carriage building probably started at the Plant during the late 1850s under the brief jurisdiction of John Coffin, the first Carriage Superintendent of the GNR, who died during 1858. The four-wheelers built at this time were primitive in terms of passenger comforts and dangerous for haulage at any speed above walking pace. Natural lighting was minimal and artificial light was provided by oil lamps, no toilet facilities existed and the basic cart-spring arrangement of sus-

pension provided a ride which was lively to say the least. As automatic power braking was years ahead in the future, all braking was done by the driver (via the locomotive) and the brakesmen along the train who did their best to stop or slow the train in a reasonable manner. Fortunately, the nature of the London-Edinburgh main line dictated that passengers must have decent rolling stock in which to spend such a long journey, especially as speeds were always increasing and better facilities were always being demanded by the travelling public. Therefore the East Coast railway companies set up a scheme for the joint operation of rolling stock by the three railways involved (the other two being the North Eastern and the North British railways), and the East Coast Joint Stock (ECJS) carriages built at Doncaster always represented the very best in carriage building to be found on the GNR. The first new train built for this service appeared in 1866 and consisted of 10 first-class carriages, five second-class, two third-class and two brakes. An interesting (but still primitive) feature was the use of 'Attock's

Patent Carriage Blocks' on the first-class stock, where rubber blocks 9in long and 1.5in thick were placed between the bodies and frames to smooth the journey somewhat. Nevertheless passenger stock — even the ECJS carriages — remained at a rather basic level until the 1870s, when Doncaster built its first sleeping carriages and also used bogies instead of simple axles below the underframes for the first time. Side corridor stock was built during the early 1880s, allowing passengers the chance to stretch their legs and also to use toilet facilities in each coach. Better lighting (both natural and artificial) and braking were gradually introduced and the long-distance traveller was eventually given a comfortable means of transport between King's Cross and Leeds, Newcastle and Edinburgh. However, the more basic four and six-wheelers continued in production for many years for use on secondary services, and many survived well into LNER and early BR days.

The 1880s saw considerable expansion at the Plant, with the gas works being enlarged in 1881 and a new

two-bay boiler shop being built in 1882 complete with plate rolls, shearing machines and hydraulically-powered riveting equipment. The foundry was improved in 1887 and 1889, and a major development took place in the latter year when the wagon shop was moved to new premises 1.75 miles south of the Plant to a site known simply as Carr. The area left empty in the Plant was used to extend the carriage shop at a time when carriages were becoming larger and heavier and needed much more time, effort and materials to be spent in order to keep up with modern developments. Carr wagon works consisted of two electrically-lit shops, supplied by three 18kW Elwell-Parker dynamos through a bank of accumula-

tors. New wagons were built in the north shop, where seven roads were placed amidst woodworking tools, wheel and axle lathes and a steam hammer. The south shop had 15 roads for repair work and also built horse-drawn road wagons, vans and drays.

Carr wagon works was built on the south-western side of the main line almost directly opposite to the famous 'Carr loco', Doncaster's motive power depot which had opened on 27 March 1876 and replaced an earlier establishment on the down side of the passenger station. At this time the depot's allocation totalled approximately 80 locomotives, the longest run being a return trip to Peterborough, usually with a Stirling 'single-wheeler'. Previous to this outburst of railway development, Doncaster Carr had been a large swamp filled with ducks and pike, and the wagon works staff train which ran daily to and from the station was always known as the 'Pike Island Flyer' or, in later years, as the 'Spikey'.

Further Developments

Doncaster's original 1848 passenger station was a temporary structure which lasted for only two years before being replaced by permanent buildings about 450yd further north. The 1848 station was a simple affair consisting of two platforms served by loops off the through running lines, and with a small locomotive depot at the south end of the up platform and a coke and water point at the northern end of the York platform. This was enlarged by 1880 to cater for the South Yorkshire traffic (Cherry Tree became a Midland goods depot and the SYR trains worked into the GNR station from 1852), the principal changes being the enlargement of the platforms to lengths of 460ft. The most significant changes took place between 1873 and 1877, when £20,000 was spent on

further enlargements which produced the basic form of the station which survives today. Three through platforms were created by placing another line along the western platform, making this an island structure for use by northbound traffic only. Two bay platforms were built into the north end of the island, and two more were placed at the south end of the single up platform. The new northbound platform was no less than 380yd long, the others being 245yd. A collection of booking offices was placed along the up platform, serving the GNR, NER, MSLR, LYR, GER and MR companies who all jostled for a share of Doncaster's lucrative passenger traffic. Extensive canopies supported by cast iron columns covered the new platforms but left the centre through roads exposed. Inconveniently the railway approaches to the north of the station were extremely cramped due to the proximity of the canal and the Great North Road (which crossed the two lines on the level at Frenchgate level crossing), and the mixture of both local and express passenger trains with the procession of coal trains plying between South Yorkshire and Scunthorpe must have produced some knotty operational problems for years on end. This problem was eventually tackled in the last years to 1914, but one wonders if the expenditure could not have been justified (say) during the last 10 years of the 19th century, when coalfield development was rapidly progressing.

The goods facilities at Cherry Tree were replaced by larger premises during the early 1880s, but the station — known as St James' station, after the nearby church — survived in passenger use for many years,

Above:
A 1947 view of Doncaster station, showing almost-new Class B1 4-6-0 No 1139 pausing with the 18.10 York-Swindon. The roof structures and colonnades of the 1873-77 rebuilding are clearly visible, and the down main platform is undergoing repair work. *J. H. Turner collection*

especially for excursion traffic and during St Leger week. Decoy marshalling yard was opened on land reclaimed from nature which had previously been used for the shooting of wild ducks, hence the unusual name for the new sidings. Meanwhile, matters at the Plant rolled on much as they had been doing since 1853, with shops being enlarged and re-equipped with better tools as the demands became even greater. The new erecting shop was built by 1891, with a capacity for 10 locomotives within the two bays serviced by two 30-ton overhead cranes provided by Craven Brothers of Manchester. A third machine shop was built in 1891, the upper and lower turneries were improved during 1895, the west carriage shop was built by 1898, and the famous Crimpsall repair shop — named after the meadow which once occupied the site — was built during 1900-01. The most modern such workshop in the country at the time, the Crimpsall could handle 100 locomotives per year within its six bays which were serviced by two 35-ton and two eight-ton cranes. A traverser connected the shop to the wheel and tender shops nearby, and coppersmiths and boilersmiths worked in some of the smaller bays.

The turn of the century conveniently marks a turning point in the development of the Plant. Up to this time progress was made mostly by enlarging the buildings or erecting new shops, but beyond this point development concentrated on using new means

of works power (principally hydraulic accumulators, compressed air and electricity) in order to increase the production capability of the entire Plant. By the end of the Victorian era, Britain was known as the 'workshop of the world', and the rapid development of engineering and manufacturing techniques at home, in the United States and in mainland Europe — particularly in Germany — had done much to alleviate the earlier reliance on very basic tools and techniques stemming from an age of sheer muscle-power. Electricity generation at the Plant started in 1899, when a small power house was built in part of the lower turnery and consisted of two 150hp Williams & Robinson vertical engines each coupled to an 88kW 2-pole dynamo. By 1901 the same makers had supplied a further 350hp/220kW set, and further enlargements brought the total capacity to 836kW by 1906. The use of electricity then spread at such a rate that larger generators were built into the Plant almost as space could be found for them; during 1910/1911 a 300kW 8-pole dynamo and 460hp four-cylinder diesel generating set was built into the old erecting shop and a smaller 240kW/three-cylinder unit was placed in a new power house at the north side of Crimpsall shop. Carr wagon works was electrified at the same time and in 1910-13 the system there was gradually modernised by using 350hp engines fired by saw-yard waste; surely an excellent method of disposal for the large amounts of off-cuts, shavings and sawdust. Hydraulic power was used extensively (a large new hydraulic riveter was installed in the boiler shop during 1907) and a central hydraulic power station had been formed in part of the forge during 1902. Two electrically driven pumps were used to keep two accumulators charged up to 1,500lb/sq in, from where the hydraulic mains took the power to the shops as required.

51

Above:
Class C13 4-4-2T No 67411 passes the control office at St James' Bridge station with a Barnsley-Doncaster local on 31 August 1954. *T. S. Walker*

Below:
A 12-coach load of empty stock is taken out of the station *en route* to Finsbury Park by Class O4/1 2-8-0 No 63677 on 22 June 1960. *P. C. H. Robinson*

The last production-engineering innovation brought into the Plant before 1914 was the introduction of drop stamping in 1907, which allowed the forging of smaller duplicate items to be done on a repeatable basis using dies, rather than having manually to produce each item individually at greater cost and with variation in tolerances. The master dies were cut using a Kendall & Gent milling and profiling machine, the blanks were heated in a Ferguson oil-fired furnace, and the stamping was done by an 'Ajax' forging machine. The smiths were still well-used, however, and two hammers (25cwt and 16cwt) were also provided.

5: Coalfield Development to 1916

The Yorkshire coalfield forms part of a much larger field which stretches from the eastern slopes of the Pennines as far as Nottingham, the Humber and the Ouse, and also reaches well into Derbyshire and towards Lincolnshire. Within this area coal has been found and worked in some form or other for many hundreds of years, starting perhaps with the simple digging of exposed coal seams in the far western areas and developing, via dozens of pits across central Yorkshire, into today's scene of a very few super-pits producing vast tonnages from coalfaces which are around 3,000ft below ground. Very briefly, the coal seams become deeper as they travel eastwards; the seams which are exposed in the west (ie those which 'outcrop') are laid on beds of millstone grit and then descend below a layer of limestone as they pass eastwards of a line roughly drawn from Pontefract to Mexborough. The Barnsley seam outcrops in the town of that name before striking deeply underground towards Selby, York, Goole and Doncaster, and the width of the seam (between 6ft and 11ft) and the quality of the fuel made exploitation well worthwhile. This seam was the basis of Doncaster's development as a coal town from the mid-1800s and continues to this day to be a prominent supplier of coal for rail haulage in the area.

Coal mining in the West Riding heartlands around Leeds, Bradford, Dewsbury and Wakefield pre-dates such activity around Doncaster by centuries, and the concealed coalfield was not exploited until Denaby Main colliery was sunk during 1863-67. (The terms 'Doncaster' and 'concealed' are used to describe that part of the coalfield where the seam is overlaid by the limestone strata mentioned earlier.) At this time it was generally thought that the depth of the seam made exploitation impossible eastwards of a line roughly followed by the East Coast main line, but that plenty of opportunity existed within the Doncaster-Worksop-Sheffield-Rotherham-Barnsley area. Rail access was well-provided in the Sheffield-Doncaster-Rotherham-Barnsley area, and several promoters quickly produced schemes for a Doncaster-Worksop link, but initially these foundered. Notable attempts were made in 1865, 1872 and 1880 and were principally orchestrated by the MR and MSLR, but were defeated by duplication, expense and the hovering uncertainty of any decent return on capital which would remain until a mine actually started producing coal from this untouched countryside.

The Hull & Barnsley Railway

After the establishment of the MSLR route from Mexborough to Thorne and Grimsby, and the

Below:
Hemsworth & South Kirby station on the Hull & Barnsley Railway's line to Cudworth, pictured in July 1965.
M. Mitchell

Above:
Class B1 4-6-0 No 61119 heads south along the WRGR line near Hampole with a string of mineral empties on 30 July 1961. The overbridge carried the H&BR South Yorkshire Junction Railway *en route* from Wrangbrook to Denaby. *P. Cookson*

Right:
The west end of Wrangbrook tunnel in July 1963, four years after closure to traffic from the east. *M. Mitchell*

MSLR/NER route to Hull via Thorne and Staddlethorpe, the Barnsley coalowners were effectively locked into a monopoly which gave these companies total control of the transport of coal for export via the Humber ports. The coalowners felt that better rates could be had if an alternative railway to Hull was built, and in March 1880 a meeting was held in Mexborough to promote the newly-formed Hull, Barnsley & West Riding Railway & Dock Co which was to 'benefit' the collieries at Denaby Main, South Kirkby, Monckton Main, Carlton, Old Oaks, Manvers Main, Roundwood, Thrybergh and Rawmarsh. Connections would be made with the MR at Cudworth, the WRGR at Hemsworth, the LYR at far-off Gowdall, the newly-opened Swinton & Knottingley joint at Moorthorpe and even to the MSLR at Stairfoot near Barnsley. Hull corporation was keen to see the NER monopoly in dock operation challenged, and accordingly backed the scheme with hard cash towards the building of Alexandra Dock. Naturally the scheme was opposed fiercely by the MSLR and NER, but the Act was granted in 1880 and construction went ahead immediately on this long railway which, after leaving Hemsworth, trekked across the countryside and climbed the Yorkshire Wolds before finally reaching Hull. It was a brave venture by the promoters, and the company had a long, hard struggle against the existing railways, especially the NER. Running from a point near Cudworth on the MR main line, this first branch of the H&BR served no purpose with respect to the Doncaster coalfield, but its promoters included the owners of Denaby Main colliery, who clearly saw future coal being moved in large tonnages from Doncaster. The H&BR was the first of many railway schemes which were to appear alongside the developing coalfield (compared to the existing Barnsley field) right up to the years of World War 1, and the importance of these early developments cannot be overlooked.

The H&BR opened to goods traffic in July 1885, and although no great engineering problems had been encountered, the line had cost about £60,000 per mile to build — a very high figure for the times. The NER immediately started a rate war which made life very hard indeed for the Hull & Barnsley, but the company was on good terms with the Midland Railway which offered to lease the H&BR in 1888 and fight its way out of the NER conflict. This was strongly opposed by Hull corporation and a myriad of smaller coalowners from seemingly all points between Worksop and Barnsley, and the H&BR was left to struggle on until some sense eventually prevailed around the turn of the century.

The Denaby company expanded during the late 1880s to exploit coal at Cadeby colliery, sunk on the opposite bank of the Don between 1889 and 1893. Denaby's chairman was once again amongst the promoters, and in 1889 a scheme was drawn up to build a line from Denaby, off the MSLR, through Sprotborough, to join the H&BR at Wrangbrook, and also to reach the GNR and GN/GE Joint Line at Bessacarr.

his was to be known as the South Yorkshire Junction Railway, based presumably on the system's connection with the former South Yorkshire line at Denaby. Cadeby coal was clearly destined to reach Hull (via the H&BR), London (via the GNR) and the GER system via the Joint Line! The scheme was lost in Parliament, but was resubmitted in far grander form during 1890 to include lines from Wath to Sprotborough and a new line direct to the NER at Thorne, and still including the H&BR connection at Wrangbrook, but only the GNR at Bessacarr. The Wath and Thorne lines were removed before the Bill went to Parliament, and the Act was granted during 1890 along with powers to negotiate working arrangements with either the H&BR or the GER. (This latter seems a strange choice, bearing in mind the deletion of the GN/GE line access from the Bill.) Only the Wrangbrook-Denaby section was built, and no connection with the MSLR at the latter place was to be put in. The H&BR agreed to work the line: goods and mineral traffic was carried from September 1894 and passen-

ger traffic — a rarity amidst such mineral lines — from 1 December via stations at Denaby, Sprotborough and Pickburn & Brodsworth. These were connected with the H&BR system as far eastwards as Carlton, the last station before the line crossed the river Ouse via a swing bridge at Drax, but passenger traffic generated by the SYJR was so meagre that its withdrawal was proposed only one year after opening and was finally removed in February 1903. The collieries at Denaby and Cadeby were the only ones served by the SYJR at its opening, and the GN/GE connection at Bessacarr was abandoned by Act of Parliament in 1897 after several unsuccessful attempts had been made to cajole various other companies (i.e. the H&BR and the GER) into building it. Brodsworth colliery was sunk between 1905 and 1907 at a point alongside the new line and the SYJR was asked to build a connection into the new pit. However, the SYJR was still virtually a colliery railway owned by the Denaby and Cadeby coalowners, who refused the request from their new competitors.

The H&BR nevertheless quickly offered their services,
and a connection was laid in by March 1906,
although a permanent layout was not established for
another four years. At the same time the GCR was
granted powers to build a connection from its line at
Denaby into the SYJR to give access all the way to
Brodsworth, so completing the MSLR/SYJR connection originally presented in the 1888 plans. The GCR
ran to Brodsworth from July 1908, just two months
after it had also opened, rather cheekily, a branch
into the colliery from the GN/GC-owned West Riding

& Grimsby line near Adwick-le-Street. Brodsworth
was well and truly a part of the Great Central system.
It was also, along with Bentley, the first of the then
super-pits which was sunk to exploit the new
coalfield, and coal was found at both locations at a
depth of approximately 1,800ft after roughly two
years' sinking work. Contrasting rather with
Brodsworth's more elaborate arrangements, Bentley
was connected into the GNR via a straightforward
north-facing spur.

The third and last branch of the Hull & Barnsley
proper was developed alongside Hickleton Main colliery from 1895 onwards. Hickleton was sunk
between 1892 and 1894 and the owners at first
requested the H&BR to build a branch to the pit, but
the Hull company refused and the colliery quickly
decided to build its own railway to Wrangbrook,
which would be called the Hull & South Yorkshire
Extension Railway. The promoters included the owners of Hickleton, Manvers Main and Wath Main collieries and also a director and the Chairman of the
H&BR! Quite how the H&BR managed to refuse the
first request from the coalowners when at least two of
their highest officers were so clearly favourable
towards the scheme is not clear, but some difficulties
had arisen between the H&BR and the SYJR owners,

and it may be that the H&BR — perhaps including a strong 'corporation' element which may have been keener to promote the company's docking business — wanted to stay out of any future wrangling. Perhaps the H&SYER's rapid plans, together with the Chairman and Director's backing, had some effect, for the H&BR quickly back-pedalled and promised all assistance with the Bill, which duly passed through Parliament in 1897. Running from Wrangbrook the line was to serve the collieries already mentioned and was also to run into Frickley colliery, then being planned, before joining the GCR near Wath. Construction began during the summer of 1899, and the line was opened for goods and passenger traffic in March and August 1902 respectively. Despite making some ambitious noises about using the line as a starting-point for building on to Nottinghamshire and Derbyshire, the connection to the GCR at Wath was never built and the line stopped dead near Wath Main colliery. The prospects of reaching further south must have tempted the H&BR sorely, for in 1898 they bought out the short-lived H&SYER company completely for a total expenditure of less than £6,500.

Passenger stations consisted of a basic platform a Wath and simple stations at Moorhouse & South Elm sall and at Hickleton & Thurnscoe, and the service lasted until April 1929 before withdrawal. Frickley

Below:
Class 8F 2-8-0 No 48473 winds a train of empties for Brodsworth along the narrow confines of the South Yorkshire Junction Railway near Pickburn on 23 July 1963. *M. Mitchell*

Right:
Coal haulage in the pre-mgr era! Class 8F 2-8-0 No 48123 leaves Pickburn and heads towards Wrangbrook with a train from Brodsworth on 8 July 1965. *M. Mitchell*

Below right:
The Wrangbrook signalman receives the single-line token from the crew of 8F 2-8-0 No 48664, which has brought a short train out of Brodsworth colliery. The loco will run round the train and then depart towards Cudworth, whose mpd supplied the ex-H&BR system motive power needs after closure east of Wrangbrook in 1959. *M. Mitchell*

Right:
The long-disused and tyre-filled H&BR cutting at Hampole in January 1991, with the electrified Leeds line in the background.
S. R. Batty

Below:
The remains of Sprotborough station, October 1990. *S. R. Batty*

Below right:
The abandoned bridge and track-bed on the H&BR's South Yorkshire Junction Railway near Cadeby tunnel, photographed in October 1990. *S. R. Batty*

colliery was sunk between 1903 and 1905 and became particularly well connected into the local railways; apart from the H&BR 1906 line there was a spur built off the Swinton & Knottingley line in 1907, and in 1909 a connection was built from the GN/GC line near Hampole to the H&BR near Moorhouse and South Elmsall, so giving access to the GNR and GCR companies.

Thus, by 1902, the Hull & Barnsley Railway consisted essentially of a main line from Hull which ended in the pit yards at Monckton and Carlton collieries near Barnsley, with branches from Wrangbrook to Denaby and Wath which had been taken over by the company after initial promotion by the coalowners. Only Brodsworth, Frickley and Denaby were directly affected by these developments over the last 15 years of the 19th century, but the age of the 'super-pit' had arrived, the concealed coalfield below Doncaster was starting to be exploited, and the H&BR was in a prime position to take advantage of all new developments. Also, by this time the company had, to a large extent, buried the hatchet with the NER and was finally making a reasonable profit in taking coal to Hull, and the years to 1914 were to give the H&BR a position of some importance in Doncaster's future railway development.

The Dearne Valley Railway

The DVR was incorporated in August 1897, at the same time as the H&SYER and, as its name suggests, was intended to serve the collieries along the Dearne valley by connecting them into the GNR and GER systems at Black Carr Junction. The principal collieries to benefit were Houghton, Hickleton, Denaby and Cadeby, with others being developed as time progressed, especially Grimethorpe, Goldthorpe, Barnburgh and Yorkshire Main at Edlington. The DVR was promoted, like the other similar lines of the 1890s, as an independent railway built by the coalowners, this time those of Carlton Main, Hickleton and Houghton. Carlton, Houghton and Denaby were relatively older pits, dating back to the 1860s/1870s, but output was increasing rapidly; Grimethorpe was sunk during the 1890s along with Hickleton and Cadeby, and the Dearne Valley pits could offer a vast tonnage of coal to any railway company prepared to take over and operate the new railway. The line was to start from a junction off the H&BR at Brierley, close to the end of the 'main' line to Cudworth, and after incorporation in 1897 several main line companies either approached or were courted by the DVR for working agreements to cover the line. The three connecting companies (the H&BR, the GNR and the GER) all showed interest, but this time a relative outsider appeared on the scene also — the Lancashire & Yorkshire Railway. Accounts of the events do vary somewhat, but it seems that many of the DVR promoters wanted the company to be bought out by the LYR right from the start. The LYR was keen to get the coal traffic, but was reluctant at first to spend any of its own money in building a connection into the DVR. Meanwhile the H&BR had signed (in 1898) a five-year mutual agreement for running powers to Grimethorpe and Houghton collieries — all this before work had hardly started on the line! By 1899 the three connecting companies were given Acts to work onto the line and during 1900 the North Eastern

got a foot in the door by being allowed to build into Hickleton (via Hickleton South Junction) from the adjacent S&K line, but the future pattern was set from 1901 when the LYR was finally persuaded to build the Dearne Valley Junction Railway from Crofton, near Wakefield, to meet the DVR proper at Shafton Junction, just south of the H&BR/DVR Brierley Junction. The LYR had taken some persuading to part with its money and the DVR had to agree to build the junction at Black Carr at its own expense. During 1902 the LYR agreed to provide £200,000 to the company (which amounted to one-third of the authorised capital) for construction of the line in return for two seats on the six-man board of directors and also the right to operate the whole line. One of the directors

was to be the Chairman of the company, and thus did the LYR end up with a railway which eventually connected with the GER system, rather as had been attempted some 40 years previously.

The DVR was opened in stages, making a rather long-winded affair out of what should have been a fairly straightforward job. The Don was crossed near Conisbrough by a magnificent 113ft-high viaduct which clearly took a long time to build, but which became the only piece of railway architectural interest to be found anywhere near Doncaster. The area's flatness obviously does not generate any great need for structures such as this, but the engineering of the DVR produced this wonderful edifice which straddles the Don at a point close by the equally impressive (but much older!) remains of Conisbrough castle. Even in its derelict 1991 condition the viaduct remains pleasant to view, and offers an industrial complement to the nearby castle.

Opening from Brierley Junction to Houghton took place in March 1902, to Hickleton (South Junction, with the S&K) in March 1903 and on to Cadeby by January 1906. At the LYR end the Dearne Valley Junction Railway was brought into use in March 1905, being over five miles in length and putting the collieries at Grimethorpe and Houghton directly in touch with the LYR main line to Goole. Hickleton and Denaby collieries were reached in February and March 1906 respectively, the latter via an LYR promoted branch which was not part of the original DVR scheme. The short Denaby-Cadeby stretch opened in August 1904 but nearly five years were to pass before

the Cadeby—Black Carr West/St Catherine's Junction section was finished. The crossing at Conisbrough viaduct consisted of 21 brick spans of 55ft each with a single lattice girder span of 150ft used for the actual crossing of the Don. The high clearance avoided any possible future problems with the owners of the Navigation should they decide to upgrade the waterway to ship canal standards in the future. (The success of the Manchester Ship Canal caused many canal owners to prepare similar plans around the turn of the century, and any such desires to turn Sheffield into an inland port would have wreaked havoc with the rebuilding of any railway bridges which did not give sufficient headway.) Once off the viaduct, eastbound trains would cross beneath the Doncaster-Rotherham road via a cutting of 70ft depth which replaced the original plan for a tunnel and so saved a considerable amount in building costs. The last openings took place in a rather untidy manner, perhaps due to difficulties with the contractors' handing-over dates. A spur from St Catherine's Junction on the South Yorkshire Joint Railway (to be described soon) to Black Carr West on the DVR was opened on 7 October 1908, and the line was opened from here to Edlington (where work was shortly to start on the sinking of Yorkshire Main colliery) on 19 October. The system was completed on 17 May 1909 with the opening from Cadeby to Edlington and the completion of the works in the Black Carr area. Black Carr West-Bessacarr used a flying junction to gain access to the GN/GE Joint line, and a similar arrangement was used from Black Carr East to reach the GNR main line at Loversall Carr. A joint LYR/GNR spur was

built from St Catherine's Junction to meet the DVR at Black Carr East, so giving northbound trains off the South Yorkshire Joint Railway access to the DVR either westwards or eastwards.

Three years later, a passenger service was started from 3 June 1912 between Wakefield (Kirkgate) and Edlington (for Balby), utilising the 'stations' at Ryhill, Grimethorpe, Great Houghton, Goldthorpe & Thurnscoe, Harlington, Denaby and Edlington (for Balby). The 'stations' were really very primitive halts, made up of a nameboard and fencing, a couple of lamps and an old coach body which had been modified for use as a waiting room! Edlington may seem a strange place at which to terminate a local passenger service after a 20.25-mile trip from Wakefield when Doncaster was so close by, but as the LYR had no direct access into the town from the DVR it clearly thought that it was not worth the trouble of trying to get into Doncaster via the southern approach. They already had access via Knottingley, and even this route could

Below:
The central girder span of Conisbrough viaduct, complete with graffiti handiwork by an army of unofficial painters who clearly have a head for heights and/or no sense of danger. *S. R. Batty*

Right:
A 'WD' 2-8-0 plods through the remains of Goldthorpe & Thurnscoe Halt. The overbridge carries the DVR above the NER/MR Swinton-Knottingley Joint line. *G. Warnes*

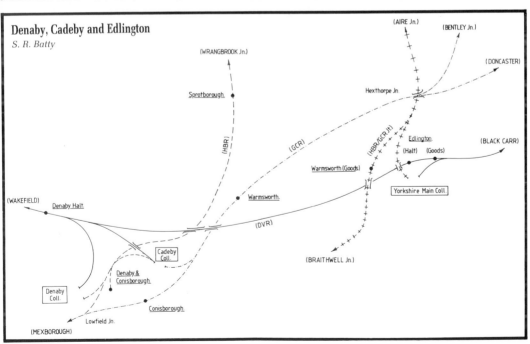

Denaby, Cadeby and Edlington

S. R. Batty

(AIRE Jn.)

(BENTLEY Jn.)

(WRANGBROOK Jn.)

(DONCASTER)

Sprotborough.

Hexthorpe Jn.

(HBR)

(GCR)

(HBR/GCR Jt.)

Edlington.

(BLACK CARR)

(Halt) (Goods)

Warmsworth (Goods)

Warmsworth.

Yorkshire Main Coll.

(WAKEFIELD)

Denaby Halt.

(DVR)

Cadeby
Coll.

(BRAITHWELL Jn.)

Denaby &
Conisborough.

Denaby
Coll.

Conisborough.

Lowfield Jn.

(MEXBOROUGH)

not compete with the much faster GN/GC Joint Don-caster-Wakefield line via South Elmsall. The DVR passenger service provided a direct link from the Dearne Valley villages it served to Wakefield, and initially the four daily return trips took approximately one hour for the journey. By 1914 the service was as below:

Wakefield Kirkgate Dep.	08.10	10.25	13.15	15.20
Edlington Dep.	09.13	11.28	14.15	16.20

An extra train left Wakefield on Saturdays only at 09.30 and returned from Edlington at 1030. Even eight years later, the service was virtually unchanged:

Wakefield Kirkgate Dep.	08.10	09.30(SO)	10.25	13.19	15.25
Edlington Dep.		09.13	10.36(SO)	11.28	14.12	16.28

The first departure from Wakefield at 08.15 on Monday 3 June 1912 carried a satisfactory number of passengers, including two policemen and four hand-cuffed prisoners due to appear at Doncaster's West Riding Court House. (One wonders why the prisoners were taken via the DVR when transport from Edlington would have been needed, and also when Westgate station was directly connected to the adjacent prison buildings.) No ceremony was performed, but Wakefield's mayor, Mr Harry White, saw off the train. Railway officials present included Inspector Noutch, Mr Law and Mr Idle, plus a few invited friends who made the train-load up to 20 passengers. An LYR rail-motor was provided, consisting of an open saloon coupled to a small 0-4-0T locomotive. Seating inside the saloon was made up of cane rattan seats, and fares were taken on the train. The driving windows in the end of the coach also made for excellent visibility for the passengers, especially when the unit was being propelled. Only three passengers boarded at Edlington for the return journey, but a rush was reported later in the day between Goldthorpe and Wakefield. Despite the line's focus being upon Wakefield, some comment was made that hopefully the local tradespeople would ensure that a connection was put in to Doncaster, but the service was little more than a basic passenger timetable grafted on top of a mineral railway which was never intended to cater for the needs of Doncaster travellers.

Contemporary descriptions of the opening were naturally devoid of the lyrical style so often found in earlier, Victorian, descriptions of such events, but mention was made of the stretches of South Yorkshire's pastoral scenery which had succumbed to colliery development. The Milnes family, who owned land around Great Houghton, had left the area where development was rapidly progressing, but the domain of Lord Halifax in the Hickleton area was as resplendent as ever, despite the ravages of Hickleton Main in the Thurnscoe area. The line's gradients were certainly noticeable, starting with a climb from Crofton to Ryhill at 1 in 92 to 1 in 178 and then a descent at 1 in 100 to 1 in 586 to Grimethorpe. Some undulation followed before climbing at 1 in 100 to Conisbrough viaduct, beyond which the line fell again to Black Carr. From here the DVR was carried over the GNR main line by a lattice girder bridge carrying double track, a smaller single-track structure

Left:
Class O4/8 2-8-0 No 63871 shunts at Yorkshire Main colliery on 13 January 1966 whilst...

Below:
... No 63653 does the job just two weeks later.
Both L. A. Nixon

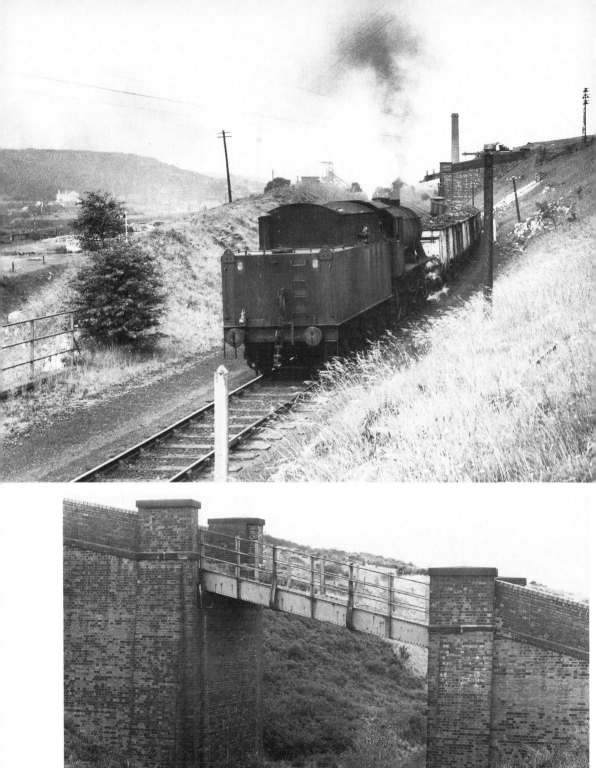

taking the line over the GNR/GER Joint line as part of the flying junction. As built, the entire railway was single-tracked, but some doubling took place from 1912 (just before the passenger service was started) to 1916 between Shafton Junction and Barnburgh, and between Goldthorpe and Denaby. The collieries at Denaby and Cadeby were both reached by the DVR, which at this point was carried on a terrace cut into the hillside above both collieries. A short length of double track was needed to cater for the sidings to both collieries, but single track was resumed as the line progressed south-eastwards towards the 1,525yd-long viaduct at Conisbrough. This was built to carry double track but always had only a single line, which

was slewed across the viaduct from one side to the other, presumably in some sort of attempt to even out the loading of the viaduct structure. (Considerable expense would have been saved if it had been built as a single-line structure in the first place.)

Edlington colliery must have been the apple of the eye of the LYR during their promotion of the DVR. This pit was promoted by the owners of Brodsworth colliery and was clearly intended to be another super-pit. Although sinking commenced in 1909, the main seam was not located until 1912, by which time the colliery had been renamed Yorkshire Main and a straightforward spur had been laid in from the DVR, using colliery waste as building material. Coal traffic along the Dearne Valley Railway quickly grew to very high levels, and the majority was despatched, not unexpectedly, via Wakefield and the LYR system to either the Leeds/Bradford area or towards Goole for ship-loading. Relatively little appears to have gone towards the GNR or GER, in spite of the comprehensive layout at Black Carr. Despite being threatened by ever-growing road competition right from the start of the passenger timetable, the LYR Hughes 0-4-0T railmotors continued in operation on the precarious passenger service right through the 1920s and 1930s — an extra evening working was even fitted in during the 1920s.

The South Yorkshire Joint Railway

This was the penultimate jointly-owned coal railway to be built in the Doncaster coalfield, and it was destined to be the most successful in terms of joint operation and length of use. It is still in use today as a

Left:
Class WD 2-8-0 No 90631 passes Cadeby colliery with a coal train heading towards Doncaster on 8 July 1965. The remains of the H&BR Denaby branch lie below the bridge on the extreme left, and the Doncaster-Sheffield (ex-SYR) line can just be seen in the background. *M. Mitchell*

Below left:
A 1990 view of the bridge above the train in the previous scene. Like all surviving DVR brickwork, it appears to be in remarkably good shape. *S. R. Batty*

Below:
A view from the bridge in October 1990. The ex-H&BR branch lies beyond the cutting to the left, and a Class 47-hauled Provincial train and a Sprinter DMU are about to pass near Conisbrough station. *S. R. Batty*

vital carrier of coal products associated mainly with only three collieries (Dinnington, Maltby and Markham Main), and at the present time no shadow appears to be cast over the line's future. Opened in 1909, the SYJR was the culmination of years of competition between both main line and independent railway companies in reaching the new coalfield, but with one very important difference — it was a truly *joint* line, conceived, built and operated for the benefit of all involved. The pattern should have been established years beforehand to put some rationalisation into the coalfield railways, but by the time the SYJR was running and making a profit it was too late to turn the clock back. Whilst the Joint line was set to survive for many years into the future, the post-1918 years and the onset of road competition were close at hand to deal some heavy blows to the earlier lines. Today's Joint line operations feed a considerable amount of traffic into Doncaster, and although the history of the SYJR is concerned largely with events in the distant areas of Worksop, Dinnington, Thurcroft and Maltby, the story is too important to be overlooked in any description of the town's railways. It is a tale of scheme and counter-scheme, of companies small and large fighting tooth and nail to corner a slice of the output from large, modern collieries planned during the early 1900s. It is also a confusing story which came to a common-sense ending in spite of years of wrangling by all concerned.

Coal measures were known to exist in what is essentially today's North Nottinghamshire coalfield in the 1870s, and some early schemes for railway access were put forward despite there being no immediate prospects of the seams being worked. At this time the area roughly bounded by Rotherham, Doncaster and Worksop was largely untouched by railways and remained extremely rural in character.

The first railway plans all failed and not a sod was turned to disturb matters, but change was inevitable. The Manchester, Sheffield & Lincolnshire Railway and the Midland Railway had co-operated in the Mansfield area, and both companies attempted to obtain Acts for lines from near Worksop to run northwards to the Swinton/Conisbrough areas. In 1890-91 the MR proposed a Shireoaks-Laughton-Dinnington railway which then forked towards both Swinton and the MSLR line near Cadeby, and the MSLR planned a Kiveton-Denaby branch, both of which never even went to Parliament. A grander scheme was then proposed, consisting essentially of the previous MR plan with further connections at Swinton and Kiveton, but this was abandoned too, mainly because of the lack of any immediate prospects of the coal being worked.

One further stillborn scheme deserves a brief mention here, if only to illustrate how the railway companies' appetites could be whetted by the prospects of thick, black seams of workable coal reserves. In 1891 the Rotherham, Blyth & Sutton Railway was granted an Act to build a railway from the GNR main line between Ranskill and Sutton to Rotherham via Styrrup, Maltby and Whiston, right across the prime sites for future colliery development. The GNR and LYR pressed the company to expand further by building another line from Maltby towards Barnsley, complete with various connections along the way into the MR, MSLR and LYR. Opposition from the MSLR saw the authorised line cut back to Swinton, but running powers over the MSLR would still give access to

Below:
The 1990 remains of the DVR near Great Houghton.
S. R. Batty

Above:
Laughton East Junction in September 1968, looking towards Thurcroft and Maltby. *M. Mitchell*

Barnsley. The LYR even made moves to use the proposed new line as a direct GNR-Huddersfield route, but the entire scheme fell by the wayside during the 1890s, once again due to the lack of any positive moves to exploit the coal reserves. Thus, after having their feet in the starting blocks since the early 1890s, the railway companies then experienced a series of false starts until the end of the century. What really pulled the trigger of the starter's pistol was the start of work in the sinking of pits at Dinnington and Silverwood during 1899/1900, by which time the main line companies (ie the GNR, MR and GCR) were extremely wary of any proposed new colliery projects. The Dinnington and Silverwood owners both approached the Midland Railway and the Great Central Railway (as the MSLR had become) to provide them with rail access, but both were initially refused and went away to build their own private railways to connect with the nearest convenient main lines.

After 10 years of failure the attitude of the GCR and MR was understandable, but their ideas were about to change rapidly. In 1899 plans were laid for the Wales-Laughton Light Railway to connect Dinnington, via a five-mile branch, to the MR and GCR near Kiveton. The Light Railway Order was granted in July 1901, after failing in an earlier attempt during the

same year owing to opposition from the Shireoaks, Laughton-Maltby Railway. This newcomer sprang up during 1900 as a GCR-backed scheme to reach Dinnington and Maltby from a new double junction on the Sheffield-Worksop line at Brancliffe, much to the disgust of the GNR which had already obtained access over the Wales & Laughton Light Railway at Dinnington. The W&LLR received their Order, but the line was not built. Instead, the colliery owners agreed to abandon the line if the SL&MR was built through to Conisbrough, very much as had been planned ten years previously. The GCR agreed with the MR to take over the SL&MR, the W&LLR was abandoned, and eyes were cast towards Conisbrough yet again. In the event, only a short section of the SL&MR was built, from Brancliffe to a point roughly midway between Dinnington and Thurcroft collieries, and this opened during 1905.

Meanwhile events had been progressing at nearby Silverwood, with sinking taking place from 1900-03 and plans being made for extending an existing colliery railway from Roundwood into the new pit after the GCR and MR had again refused to build any new lines. The collieries' Roundwood & Dalton Colliery Railway was opened in 1901, and had been built to heavy mineral standards in anticipation of being ultimately taken over by the main line companies. In 1903 plans were made to enlarge considerably this little system by the promotion of the Rotherham, Maltby & Laughton Railway, which was intended to start from junctions with the GCR and MR lines near

Roundwood, pass the Silverwood spur and then sweep southwards (alongside an already authorised H&BR line) via Thurcroft to meet the SL&MR at a site to be called Anston Junction. The GCR still could not be persuaded to take over, largely due to the reluctance of the Midland Railway, the GCR's partner in several joint mineral lines, to become involved. The Hull & Barnsley was not so shy, however, and quickly agreed to having part of its line used by the RM&LR in return for running agreements.

Whereas the GCR and the MR had been slow off the mark in reaching the two new collieries, the North Eastern Railway and the Hull & Barnsley Railway were much quicker to see the opportunities presented and lost no time in making plans. The NER effort came to very little, but the H&BR made its presence felt. This latter company, during 1900, proposed to build a line from near Hickleton & Thurnscoe station (on the still-under-construction Wrangbrook-Wath branch) to Maltby and to Dinnington colliery, with a branch from Swinton passing close by Silverwood on its way to Aldwarke Main and Rotherham. Close to Dinnington another spur was to meet with the then-proposed Wales & Laughton Light Railway, which of course was never built as a result of subsequent developments. The NER's proposals were even grander, consisting of a line from just north of Haxey, on the Isle of Axholme Light Railway, running through Bawtry and Tickhill to a point near Roche Abbey where the line forked towards Silverwood via

Maltby and to Dinnington. At this point the two companies realised that such expensive and highly-competitive schemes would lead them both into desperate situations, where vast amounts of time, effort and money would be expended towards very little profit. Consequently, the plans were withdrawn from the 1901 Parliamentary session, for resubmission in more rational forms during the following year. The events of 1902 led to the formation of the South Yorkshire Joint Railway Committee and the final connection of Silverwood, Thurcroft and Dinnington collieries into the new railway.

The H&BR revised proposal was a much simpler railway than that of 1901, still commencing at Hickleton & Thurnscoe and going via Denaby, Braithwell and Thurcroft to end in a junction with the SL&MR at Laughton East. Dinnington was served and a branch was laid towards Maltby, but the earlier plans to reach Swinton, Aldwarke and Rotherham were abandoned. The H&BR Act was granted in 1902. The NER made alternative plans with its old ally the LYR, and produced a scheme to connect the three colliery sites with the NER main line via a flying junction at Shaftholme and also with the LYR via a branch to Askern. The Hull line was to be joined via a branch to a junction near Thorne, and the LYR's Dearne Valley line was to be reached from Loversall Carr, making what would have been a very interesting layout at Black Carr! Two further entrants appeared for the 1902 session, the GCR/MR joint bid and the GNR last-

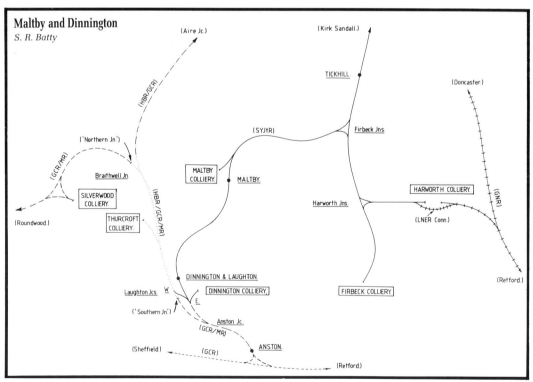

Maltby and Dinnington

S. R. Batty

(Aire Jc.)

(Kirk Sandall.)

TICKHILL.

(Doncaster.)

(HBR/GCR)

('Northern Jn.')

(SYJtR)

Firbeck Jns.

(GCR/MR)

Braithwell Jn.

MALTBY COLLIERY.

MALTBY.

HARWORTH COLLIERY.

(GNR)

SILVERWOOD COLLIERY.

(HBR./GCR./MR)

Harworth Jns.

(Roundwood.)

THURCROFT COLLIERY.

(LNER Conn.)

(Retford.)

DINNINGTON & LAUGHTON.

Laughton Jcs. W

DINNINGTON COLLIERY.

FIRBECK COLLIERY.

('Southern Jn.') E

Anston Jc.

(GCR/MR)

(Sheffield)

(GCR)

ANSTON.

(Retford.)

Above:
The former Laughton East Junction has now been abolished and traffic is controlled from Dinnington Junction. Illustrated at the Thurcroft branch is Class 56 No 56022 waiting as No 56006 takes a train of empties towards Dinnington and Worksop. *S. R. Batty*

ditch attempt to get into the new coalfield after being on the losing end of the W&LLR affair. The former's bid was for a line from Laughton to the GC main line at Kirk Sandall, passing close to Maltby and through Wadworth *en route*, and which, in the new spirit of co-operation which had finally emerged, they were quite prepared to share with the NER, LYR and GNR. The GNR's proposal rather smacked of desperation, involving connections from Scrooby and Loversall (yet more confusion at Black Carr) to a junction at Tickhill, thence to Dinnington with a branch to Maltby. Such a scheme flew directly in the face of the rational approach which had emerged towards mineral railways over the previous year, and it seems that the GNR had no real conviction over this planned railway and stated that it would probably be withdrawn from Parliament. This was done during the 1902 session, and marked the end of a rather uncharacteristic course of events for the Great Northern, which was a past master at buying up small independent railways in order to gain access to lucrative traffic. Perhaps its recent expenditure in the West Riding, around the notoriously difficult Queensbury area, had drained the company's balances too far to allow any adventures in the new coalfield.

At the start of the 1902 session the five companies involved in the new lines (ie including the GNR at that stage) clearly stated to the Select Committee that they were entirely in favour of joint undertakings being established for the promotion of further mineral railways. The way was open for the Joint Line Committee to be formed, but this took place in a long-winded way which only Parliamentary matters seem capable of achieving. Firstly, the NER/LYR and GCR/MR plans were approved together in July 1902. The former was to build a shortened railway (without the Shaftholme and Thorne connections or the GNR spurs at Loversall) from Laughton through Maltby to Kirk Sandall, connecting only with the DVR at Black Carr. The latter was to build barely a mile of railway onwards to Kirk Sandall Junction, on the GCR main line. Then came the long-windedness: there were statements in both Acts that a *joint* line should be built from the powers given by *both* Acts, and this was finally sanctioned by the South Yorkshire Joint Railway Act of the following year. This provided for the NER/LYR line to be built largely as per the 1902 Act, and for a slightly altered layout at Kirk Sandall Junction. The five companies involved would set up a joint committee to build and operate the new line, each supplying two directors. Despite being left on the sidelines during the SYJR affair, the GNR was

Right:
Class 58 No 58019 waits for signals at Maltby Colliery South. *S. R. Batty*

Below:
A loaded mgr train crosses Brookhouse viaduct towards Doncaster on 11 October 1990. *S. R. Batty*

connected via a Low Ellers-Potteric Carr line and a short-lived spur from St Catherine's to Down Decoy sidings.

At the Dinnington end of the line, the 1903 Act resulted in several jointly-owned stretches of line being transferred to the new joint company. The principal changes concerned the H&BR projected route from Hickleton to Laughton East and the RM&LR's plans for a line from Thrybergh to Anston. The latter route passed very close by the planned H&BR line,

and the Hull company was only too pleased to accept the RM&LR idea of connecting the two systems together at Braithwell and Laughton by what became known as the Northern and Southern junctions respectively. Although the GCR had earlier refused the RM&LR's offers of a take-over, it was unhappy at seeing the H&BR gain control and quickly stepped in to arrange joint ownership at the last minute. In fact the GCR did quite well for itself during these 1905 negotiations, whereby the Braithwell-Laughton line

South Yorkshire Joint Line
Correspondence, 1905. *T. S. Walker*

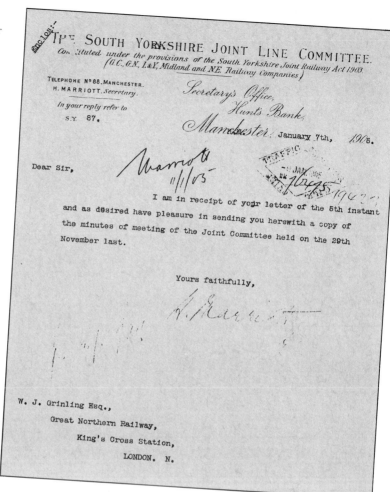

THE SOUTH YORKSHIRE JOINT LINE COMMITTEE.

Constituted under the provisions of the South Yorkshire Joint Railway Act 1903
(G.C., G.N., L.&Y., Midland and N.E. Railway Companies)

TELEPHONE Nº 88. MANCHESTER.
H. MARRIOTT. *Secretary.*

In your reply refer to
S.Y. 87.

Secretary's Office,
Hunts Bank,
Manchester, January 7th, 1905.

Dear Sir,

I am in receipt of your letter of the 5th instant and as desired have pleasure in sending you herewith a copy of the minutes of meeting of the Joint Committee held on the 29th November last.

Yours faithfully,

W. J. Grinling Esq.,
Great Northern Railway,
King's Cross Station,
LONDON. N.

Left:
Class 58 No 58038 brushes aside the trees on Wadworth Carr with an empty train bound for Maltby on 11 October 1990. *S. R. Batty*

became a joint GCR/HBR property (with the Midland taking a share from 1907), the remainder of the RM&LR (from Thrybergh to Northern Junction and from Anston to Southern Junction) becoming a GCR/MR line, and the GCR having the option of buying a share of the H&BR Braithwell-Thurnscoe planned line. All was finalised by 1907 when the H&BR's planned line (authorised since 1902) from Hickleton was largely abandoned, and only the southern half, the Braithwell to Laughton section, was agreed to be built by a joint H&BR/GCR/MR company.

Broadly speaking, the railways around the Dinnington area can be considered physically as two connected systems. The SL&MR lines from Brancliffe, the RM&LR-promoted lines at Laughton and Braithwell, and the GCR/H&BR/MR, line formed one system which worked directly into Thurcroft and Silverwood collieries and had access to Dinnington via a branch from Anston; and the SYJR line connected Doncaster directly with Maltby colliery and also with Dinnington via the SYJR-owned spur into the colliery

from Dinnington Colliery Junction. The SL&MR Brancliffe-Dinnington colliery line was built by the Glasgow firm of Mitchell Brothers between 1902 and 1905, and the Thrybergh-Braithwell-Laughton-Anston section was laid by Henry Lovatt of Wolverhampton between February 1907 and October 1909, when the whole system was opened for goods traffic. Double track was used throughout, except for some small connections near Roundwood.

The South Yorkshire Joint line itself was built by the Leeds contractor Whitaker Brothers, which started work in October 1906. The line climbed away from St Catherine's Junction all the way to Dinnington, and was mostly a single-track affair with only the occasional double-track section being laid at congested areas such as Kirk Sandall, Low Ellers, Maltby and Dinnington. A passing loop was put in at Tickhill station. The line was opened to goods traffic from 1 January 1909, having cost the joint owners almost £240,000 to build. (The SL&MR/RM&LR/H&B/GCR/MR system had cost approximately £190,000.) As built, the Joint line finished at an end-on junction with the SL&MR at Dinnington Junction, with the colliery branch trailing in immediately north, but a second connection was built by the Joint Committee between Laughton East and West Junctions in 1911, principally to gain access to Thurcroft colliery which was then being developed. Dinnington and Silverwood were producing coal from 1904, Maltby from 1910 and Thurcroft from 1913. The Joint line arrangements worked quite well, apart from some difficulty caused by the LYR which led to legal action being taken by the GCR. The LYR had access to the line by virtue of its association with the NER during the line's promotion, and it seems the company could not wait for the line's official opening before it set about hauling coal from Dinnington along the Joint line and onto the DVR via Black Carr from October 1908! Relations with the GCR deteriorated, and there followed a great deal of bickering regarding the LYR's refusal to handle any mineral traffic off the GCR. The matter was eventually settled in 1910, rather to the GCR's disadvantage.

In response to local pressure but against the better judgement of the operating companies, a passenger service was run along the Joint line between Doncaster and Shireoaks from 1 December 1910. The previous summer had seen two excursion trains run from Dinnington and both had been very popular (one was a miners' trip to a Doncaster rally, the other a Sunday-school trip to Cleethorpes), but the authorities provided only four trains per day each way and these had to run within a 12hr operating period for

signalbox-manning purposes. These strange and constricting arrangements could give only a very poor service, and from October 1911 the timetable was reduced to three trains each way daily. Initially the trains were provided and worked equally by the GNR and GCR, but the GNR pulled out completely with the reduction in service and left the GCR to soldier on alone. Stations were built at Anston, Dinnington & Laughton, Maltby, and Tickhill & Wadworth, but a suggestion for a station by Doncaster racecourse was dismissed by the GNR, as it felt it was doing a perfectly good job in handling race traffic at the main line station. Return trips were also operated daily between Doncaster and Maltby for the benefit of the miners employed there, the six daily trains running to coincide with the shift change times. A similar service from Worksop was never operated, and the collieries at Dinnington and Thurcroft apparently never had any workmen's service at all. The miners' trains were withdrawn at the start of World War 1, and later

Right:
Class O2/2 2-8-0 No 63937 brings a loaded coal train away from the Maltby direction and prepares to head for Doncaster at Firbeck Junction on 27 July 1963. *M. Mitchell*

Below right:
Firbeck Junction on 27 March 1990, showing Class 58 No 58027 taking a train of empties towards Doncaster. *S. R. Batty*

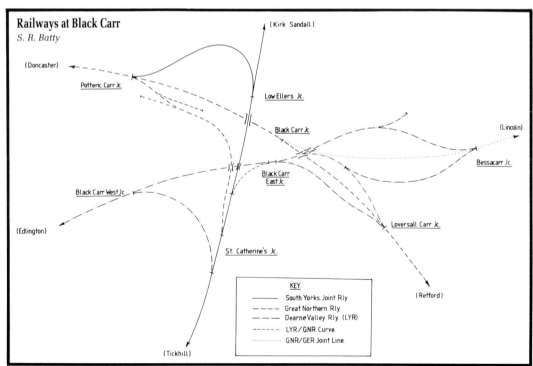

Railways at Black Carr
S. R. Batty

(Kirk Sandall.)

(Doncaster)

Potteric Carr Jc.

Low Ellers Jc.

Black Carr Jc.

(Lincoln)

Bessacarr Jc.

Black Carr East Jc.

Black Carr West Jc.

(Edlington)

Loversall Carr Jc.

St. Catherine's Jc.

(Tickhill)

KEY.

(Retford)

———— South Yorks. Joint Rly.
– – – – Great Northern Rly.
–·–·– Dearne Valley Rly. (LYR)
–··–··– LYR/GNR Curve.
············ GNR/GER Joint Line.

Class 47 No 47201 brings an engineers' train off the SYJR at Potteric Carr Junction on 30 April 1990. *S. R. Batty*

the public passenger service was stopped as part of the large programme of train service cuts made in 1917. Re-opening took place in 1920 with two trains daily running between Doncaster and Worksop, but this lasted barely two years before withdrawal in March 1922. However, Lord Scarbrough was the principal landowner in the area, and he continually reminded the SYJR Committee of the various agreements which had been made regarding the maintaining of a passenger service over his estates, especially relating to keeping Maltby station open for passenger traffic. Therefore another re-opening took place in July 1927, again with only two trains daily, but this was reduced to just one train between Maltby and Worksop from July 1929, and even his Lordship had to agree that this was practically useless. Passenger services finally ceased from 2 December 1929.

This manner of operation could perhaps be seen as justification of the SYJR's original doubtful attitude towards passenger services, but it does seem that no effort was ever made to provide a useful and viable service. During several coal strikes which took place from 1912 to 1926 the line was closed completely, and this period saw rapid growth in the competing forms of road transport provided by trams, trolley-buses and motor-buses. It also seems the GNR was not keen to have any more local traffic squeezed into Doncaster station, and made its attitude quite clear whenever the service was discussed. Even when Markham Main colliery was being sunk the GNR adopted a very 'wait and see' attitude, preferring to let developments take their course before agreeing to having a small station built in the Armthorpe area. As events at Markham turned out, this was indeed the best course to be followed.

The Doncaster Avoiding Line

To say that Doncaster station had become a bottleneck by the turn of the century was a polite understatement. Traffic to and from Leeds, York, Hull and Grimsby was very effectively throttled by the Frenchgate level crossing immediately north of the station, where just *two* running lines were available to accommodate all the freight and passenger traffic using this end of the station. Conditions at the southern end of the station were much easier, with the St James' Junction/Bridge Junction/South Yorkshire Junction area coping adequately. As long ago as 1865 the bridge over the GNR/South Yorkshire Railway lines at Hexthorpe had been extended by two arches above four new running lines into Hexthorpe goods yard, to cater for the coal traffic being dealt with from the Swinton direction. In the same year Carr wagon sidings were opened on a 42 acre site on both sides of the line beyond Balby Bridge, where 400 empties could be sorted on the down side and 700 on the up side. The sidings were built purely to handle coal traffic, and despite there being plenty of space around the Carrs, the various necessary conflicting movements across the main line must have caused the occasional problem or two. Access to Carr wagon sidings was originally via junctions with the main line

Below:
BR Class 9F 2-10-0 No 92190 heads an up freight along the ECML past Black Carr during 1962. The South Yorkshire Joint Line passes over the main line on the bridge at the rear of the train. *J. H. Turner collection*

Above:
The GCR avoiding line and the GCR/H&BR Joint line met in a junction at Sprotborough, just north of the river Don. The Joint line fell into disuse during the 1940s, but the northern end remained usable, to a varying extent, until well into the 1970s. Here a Class 31 hauls a northbound coal train along the avoiding line past the site of the junction during 1975, with the Joint line visible in the background. *C. P. Boocock*

just north of Balby bridge, and proposals were made at the time to rebuild this into a girder structure which would give room for future expansion and also improve the local signalling arrangements, but the scheme was not pursued.

With traffic being well-accommodated at the southern end of the station area, the Frenchgate level crossing was tackled during 1909-11 by the building of North Bridge, a large brick-built multi-arched road viaduct which took the Great North Road (now the A638) above the railway. This obviously did a great deal to eliminate road traffic problems in the area and eased the GNR's problems by doing away with the level crossing, but track capacity was not increased and the same two lines remained as before. Two extra double-track bridges were laid over the Don at this time, but due to the succession of wars and depressions about to be unleashed these were not brought into use until 1949 — *40 years* afterwards.

Meanwhile, the Great Central Railway was busily expanding from Manchester to Immingham, carrying large amounts of coal in ever-increasing trainloads. Thus by 1900 the GCR was hauling coal, lime and iron ore to the steelworks at Scunthorpe and was building up the export coal trade from Immingham. What was to become the Wath marshalling yard was soon to be planned, to meet the traffic needs, and the port facilities at Immingham were to be greatly expanded to cope with the ever-increasing export coal business. When these two projects were finished (Wath yard opened in 1907 and the new Immingham docks were formally opened by King George V and Queen Mary in July 1912), the extra traffic created would be colossal, and Doncaster would be right in the middle. What was to be done? The idea of sending such traffic flows along the ex-South Yorkshire line, through the station and out via the single northern exit was a non-starter, and so the GCR made plans to build its own Doncaster avoiding line running from Hexthorpe Junction (actually situated in Sprotborough) on the South Yorkshire line to Bentley Junction on the Thorne line, a total length of just 3.75 miles. The necessary Act was obtained in 1903, but several years of generally poor trade conditions throughout the country led to the line being shelved until 1908, when in March of that year the contract was let to Logan & Hemingway. Work started during the following month and the line was completed just over two years later, being opened for goods traffic from 18.00 on 25 July 1910. The line was examined by a Board of Trade inspector on 28 July prior to being used by some Bank Holiday passenger traffic shortly afterwards.

This avoiding line was designed by the GCR's Chief Engineer, C.A. Rowlandson, its main features being the large amount of bridging built along its 3.25-mile length. Principal amongst these was the girder structure which crossed the Don, the WR&G line to Leeds and the GNR main line north of the station, where four skewed spans carried the line 42ft above river level. The river was also crossed just after the line left Hexthorpe Junction, using a much simpler lattice-girder structure. At Hexthorpe and at Newton, two short cuttings were dug out, and the entire line involved the removal of 750,000cu yd of spoil (most of the line was built on an embankment) and the construction of 13,000cu yd of brickwork. The fact that construction was carried out promptly and the contract was finished on time, drew some favourable comment at the opening. This new line was undoubtedly a great success in keeping Doncaster's station free of a great deal of heavy freight traffic, and this continues to be the case during the 1990s. (Passenger traffic has used the line very occasionally over the years, mainly excursion traffic heading towards Cleethorpes.) Local comment at the time suggested that the line need not have been built if the North Bridge scheme had been made sufficiently large to

allow enough tracks to be laid north of the station, but the station itself would still have been grossly overloaded.

The Hull & Barnsley/Great Central Joint Railway

This coalfield mineral line was the last railway to be constructed on such a scale in the Doncaster area. It was a joint undertaking built to tap existing collieries in the Dinnington area, to connect into the new mines at Brodsworth, Bullcroft and Bentley, and, most importantly, with an eye on the future, the sinkings expected to be made in the Pollington and Sykehouse area towards Snaith. Coal reserves in the Snaith area had been proved during the early years of the century, and several companies were ready to build new lines to reach the expected colliery sites. Fortunately, as with the SYJR story, common sense prevailed and extensive running powers were granted, but fate took a hand and gave the line a very short life of only limited usefulness.

The race to reach these collieries began in 1908, when the NER made proposals to build from Shaftholme Junction towards Bentley and Brodsworth and the H&BR abandoned its Thurnscoe-Conisbrough scheme of 1902 in favour of building a new line from Gowdall to Braithwell. This line would serve Bullcroft and Bentley mines and would also have a short spur to a new passenger station to be built between Bentley village and Doncaster. The NER proposals came to nothing, although the company hoped to obtain some running powers over the

Above:
Class 47/4 No 47520 passes Hexthorpe Junction with the 07.40 Newcastle-Weymouth on 28 July 1990. The rubble to the right of the locomotive marks the infilling of the former GCR/H&BR tunnel below the line. *S. R. Batty*

Left:
Class 31/2 No 5547 hauls a train of flat wagons off the avoiding line at Hexthorpe Junction and heads towards Sheffield on 14 August 1970. *T. G. Flinders*

H&BR line when it was finally built. The H&BR estimated its line would cost nearly £500,000 to build, but there was no shortage of partners willing to buy a share of the scheme. The North Eastern was granted extensive powers, including a branch to Bullcroft and Bentley and access to the new station at York Road, but the company declined the offer of a one-third share of a joint operating company. At this point the GCR stepped in quickly, demanding that it should be offered similar terms as recompense for the loss of the rights it would have enjoyed over the now scuppered Thurnscoe line. Both companies went to Parliament with their joint Bill, and approval was given

in August 1909. Barely 12 months later, the Midland Railway came along and offered £250,000 towards the line in return for running powers, a proposal which was accepted quickly. Although running powers were granted by the joint HBR/GCR committee to the MR, NER and GNR, none of these were exercised and several connections to collieries and adjacent lines were also planned but failed to materialise. Those connections which were built were sanctioned by various Acts up to 1914, and some were the result of earlier H&BR or GCR schemes which had been authorised a few years previously. The branch from Bullcroft Junction (which was close by the hamlet of

Right:
Doncaster Junction signalbox in process of demolition, Christmas 1971. The box controlled access from the GCR/H&BR Joint line to York Road station and sidings. Despite having all signalling equipment removed, the line saw occasional use after this date.
T. G. Flinders

Below:
The Joint line's girder bridge crossing of the Don, just north of its tunnel below the GCR main line at Hexthorpe Junction. The bridge is now used as part of a footpath.
S. R. Batty

Shaftholme) to the colliery was slightly altered by an Act of 1912 to give an approach via the ex-WR&G line from Stainforth to Adwick; a curve from this line to the Leeds-Doncaster line was eventually built under a GCR Act of 1907; Bentley colliery was reached by a forked junction from the joint line by an H&BR Act of 1913; Brodsworth was connected to the Doncaster-Leeds (ex WR&G) line by a north-facing connection authorised by a further GCR Act of 1907; a south-facing spur was put into York Road station by an H&BR 1914 Act; and finally Yorkshire Main colliery at Edlington was reached by a short line which was authorised along with the main line in 1909.

Construction of the main line from Aire Junction to Braithwell Junction was started by Logan & Hemingway in 1911, after long delays had been caused by the Aire & Calder Navigation's insistence on a lifting bridge being provided for the crossing of the canal near Pollington. This was actually built as such but without the equipment for driving the lifting gear, which was to be installed only if the ship canal proposals of the time came to fruition, and then only after all other bridges had been dealt with! The outbreak of war in August 1914 and the slippage of cuttings near Warmsworth delayed the opening until 1916. Although level from Aire Junction to Doncaster, some steep climbing was then encountered on the way to Braithwell Junction. Apart from the canal bridge at Pollington, the only other work of any significance was a three-section girder bridge across the Don at Hexthorpe. To the north of this was a junction layout allowing access to the GCR avoiding line in both directions, and to the south of the river the line burrowed under the GCR line through a deep cutting. Stations were built at Warmsworth, Doncaster (York Road), Thorpe-in-Balne, Sykehouse and Snaith & Pollington, the latter three being intended to serve the expected colliery housing developments in the area. Four years of warfare followed by over 15 years of depression saw off any prospects for the new coalfield, and the line was used only as a means of access to Bullcroft, Bentley and Yorkshire Main collieries. The stations never saw a single passenger, and the York Road buildings did not progress beyond the goods shed stage. Even the three pits had alternative exits already in place (Bullcroft onto the ex-WR&G lines, Bentley onto the GNR main line, and Yorkshire Main onto the Dearne Valley Railway), leaving the new joint line with a very insecure future almost from its opening.

Further Colliery Development to 1916

As already mentioned, Bentley colliery was one of the first to exploit the concealed coalfield and sinking commenced in 1905. The GNR built a branch off its main line to the colliery at this time, several years before the H&BR/GCR connection was even planned. Coal was reached in 1907-08, after considerable trouble had been encountered because of underground

Below:
Braithwell Junction in September 1968, showing rusted, overgrown tracks and the remains of the signalbox which had been reduced to ashes by vandals. *M. Mitchell*

The Great Northern Railway,
Engineers' Office,
Kings Cross, London, 22nd April, 1911.
N.

TELEPHONE
NO 3200 NORTH.

TELEGRAPHIC ADDRESS,
"TRACTRIX, LONDON."

9067

BENTLEY COLLIERY: COAL BELONGING TO LADY
BATTIE WRIGHTSON.

Dear Sir,

I have considered the enclosed letter and tracing from Mr. Embleton, the Mining Engineer to Lady Battie Wrightson, with Mr. Rowley, and we have come to the conclusion that in view of the distance this estate is from the shafts of the Bentley Colliery, and the importance of the junction to the Railway Company, it is not advisable at the present time to grant any easement or means of access to the coal under the areas marked "A", "B", and "C", on the plan accompanying Mr. Embleton's letter dated 14th February 1911.

If you agree to this decision and will let me know I will inform Mr. Embleton.

Yours faithfully,

Oliver Bury Esq.

water courses. And even greater problems were caused by hidden rivers at nearby Bullcroft, where vast amounts of water were found soon after sinking started in 1908. Eventually coal was reached in late 1911, but only after the water had been dealt with by a combination of very powerful electrically driven pumps and the use of large-scale freezing techniques which allowed the shafts to be lined and the water held back.

The colliery was situated just north of the ex-WR&G lines between Adwick and Skellow Junctions and a spur was built from the latter into the colliery, facing towards Stainforth, presumably at the same time as the GCR Skellow-Carcroft curve was built in 1908. The later HBR/GCR joint line left Bullcroft junction and then crossed above the WR&G line before entering the colliery from the eastern side, ie facing opposite the earlier spur from the WR&G. This branch was two miles long, starting from a point just north of the connection from Bullcroft junction towards Bentley colliery.

Nearby Hatfield Main colliery, near Stainforth, was built just north of the GCR line from Doncaster to Thorne, between Stainforth and Thorne Junctions. Sinking took place between 1911 and 1916 with delays being caused by wartime problems, and rail access was a straightforward matter of building in from the adjacent GCR line. Running powers were granted to the GNR, NER, LYR and even the MR by virtue of the 1902 agreement between the companies that such branches should be operated for the mutual benefit of all concerned. As events turned out, Hatfield Main's output was to be of most benefit to the nearby Stainforth & Keadby Canal Co.

Doncaster's last colliery to start commercial production during the 1914-18 period was Rossington Main, situated in a rural area which had slumbered on peacefully since completion of the main line to Retford in 1849. The mine was sunk from 1912 to 1916 and the GNR was quick off the mark (as it had been at Bentley) in obtaining an Act to build a one-mile branch from its main line into the colliery, and this was in use by 1912. The GNR acted purely on its own behalf, despite the 1902 agreement, and so the SYJR applied for powers to reach the pit during 1913, but its scheme failed.

Left:
Class O4/7 2-8-0 No 63661 leaves Bullcroft Colliery with a short trainload on 23 April 1963. *T. S. Walker*

Below:
A Class 142 DMU forming the 14.52 Doncaster-Scunthorpe passes Hatfield colliery on 16 July 1990. The rapid-loading mgr bunker had been disused for some time by this date. *S. R. Batty*

The Last Collieries

Doncaster's last four collieries to be sunk were all planned before 1914, but none produced any coal until the mid-1920s. The delays were mostly due to wartime problems, but other circumstances lengthened these to almost spectacular proportions. The pits concerned were Thorne, Markham Main, Firbeck and Harworth, the first of these having a story which has yet to reach a conclusion after almost *90 years* of problems.

Trial boring at Thorne took place in 1902 but coal was not proved until 1908 at a depth of over 900yd. The seam was expected to yield about 1.5 million tons per year, but by 1910 the sinking operation was in trouble due to inrushes of water. Pumping and freezing were again used as had been done at Bullcroft, but by 1914 very little progress had been made and coal was not expected to reach the surface before 1918. The war stopped all work for the duration, and after re-starting in 1919 coal was eventually worked from early 1925.

A simple branch was laid into the colliery by the NER during 1908/09, with access being from the Goole direction along the Thorne line. At this time the Lancashire & Yorkshire Railway had plans for reaching eastwards beyond Goole along the south bank of the Humber to create a new port which would be easier for shipping traffic to reach, and the colliery was believed to have figured largely in these plans. It would certainly have made sense for the LYR to build a short stretch of flat railway to a mod-ern wharf if it was confident of capturing the large output of the new mine, but nothing came of the scheme. After coal production started the colliery company went to Parliament in 1926 with a Bill to build a railway to a new wharf which it intended to construct on the Ouse at Swinefleet, much as the LYR had sought before 1914. Strong opposition came from all corners and the Bill was withdrawn after talks with the Aire & Calder Navigation produced an agreement for handling the coal at Goole. Coal production settled down to a consistently high output over the following 30 years, but greater problems were on the way which would see the rail connection removed, despite the colliery remaining technically open.

Markham Main (or Armthorpe) colliery was the result of test borings carried out in 1908 around the Cantley area, which proved the reserves around the racecourse area of the town. Doncaster Corporation leased the mineral rights in order to profit from the royalties to be paid on the coal produced, and sinking started near Armthorpe in 1913. The South Yorkshire Joint Railway agreed to put in a temporary connection in 1916, which was completed during the following year. A passenger station was considered at the time but, not surprisingly, was rejected by the Joint Committee. After the experiences with the Doncaster-Shireoaks service and the wartime difficulties of the day, the committee's reluctance is hardly surprising. On top of this the colliery development had all but stopped in 1914. Some problems had emerged with the various boreholes which had led to the pit-head site being altered, and there was still no

GNR Royal Train Notice, 1906.
T. S. Walker

GREAT NORTHERN RAILWAY.

Circular No. 20,903a.

INSTRUCTIONS

to Station Masters, Inspectors, Engine Drivers, Guards, Platelayers,

Signalmen, and others concerned.

JOURNEY OF

His Majesty the KING

AND SUITE

From OLLERTON to ADVIE
(L. D. & E. C.)   (G. N. of S.)

ON

MONDAY, 17th SEPTEMBER, 1906.

NOTE. These Instructions must be kept strictly private, and must only be communicated to those persons in the service of the Company who, in the discharge of their duty, require to know and act upon them; and those persons must not give any information whatever to anyone respecting the hours or other arrangements set forth in these Instructions.

Below left:
A modern headgear assembly stands alongside one of the original 1910 buildings at Thorne colliery. Despite a successful run from 1925 to 1956, problems of flooding, repairs, investment policy and cut-backs have now kept the mine inactive (but not quite abandoned) for 35 years. *S. R. Batty*

Below:
A view of Class O4/7 No 63661, seen preparing to leave Markham Main colliery with a coal train on 14 July 1964. *T. S. Walker*

firm estimate of when coal would be reached. Sinking was finally restarted in 1922 after trade recovered a little and labour problems eased, and coal was reached two years later. The full connection to the former SYJR system (by this time a joint LNER/LMSR railway), complete with sidings and headshunts, was completed during 1924 and was controlled by Markham Sidings signalbox. By this time the passen-

Above:
Ex-ROD 2-8-0 No 63813 gets away from Markham Main with a loaded train during the 1960s. *T. S. Walker*

Below:
Class 37 No 37239 leaves Markham Main yard with a Speedlink coal train on 18 September 1990. The train will run forward, reverse onto the Joint Line in the background and then depart for Doncaster. *S. R. Batty*

ger operations at the far end of the Joint line were on their last legs, and plans for Armthorpe station were consigned to the realms of history.

Firbeck Main and Harworth collieries were contemporaries of each other, with both being linked to the SYJR by new lines from Firbeck Junction and Harworth also having a line to the GNR at Scrooby. The first moves for Firbeck's rail connection were made between 1911 and 1914, and were almost a repeat performance of the chaotic years prior to 1902. The mining company approached the GNR and GCR to build the necessary connections, both companies refused and the directors then formed their own railway company to do the job themselves. And what a railway they had in mind — almost a repeat order of the schemes which had been planned at various times since the 1870s to penetrate this rural area! The line was to leave the GCR and MR near Shireoaks, pass Firbeck and the proposed Harworth site and end in flying junctions with the GNR between Scrooby and Bawtry. Opposition was aroused from the Joint Committee as well as the GCR, GNR and MR in their own rights, but the Bill went to Parliament in 1915 — in the middle of the war — and was progressing well before the promoters thought again and approached the SYJR for a satisfactory agreement. This re-think was probably brought about by recent developments at nearby Harworth, where sinking had started in 1913, a year after work began at Firbeck. The owners there wanted a connection from the GNR (which had been surveyed in 1910 and passed to Parliament in 1911 — more fast work by the Great Northern!) and

extension through to the SYJR line. The GNR branch was authorised and two years later, in 1913, the SYJR partners promoted a line from Firbeck Junction to Harworth which was presented to Parliament by the NER on behalf of the Joint Committee and duly passed in 1914. The GNR was also to be allowed to build a short connection into the SYJR branch.

It was at this point that the Firbeck owners approached the SYJR, and it seems odd that Parliament should have gone so far with two mineral railway schemes which could clearly have been rationalised into a common system which would have served everyone's needs. The SYJR did away with the Worksop-Bawtry proposal and substituted an application for a Light Railway Order to build a line from Harworth Junction to the colliery site which would allow the contractors to move materials, etc, as required — sinking was some years away and would have to wait for the war to end before any serious efforts were made. This Order was granted during 1916, but no work was started. A temporary line from the GNR to Harworth was built by 1914 but the permanent line was installed by the LNER during 1924. Sinking was resumed in 1919 and coal was reached in 1923, but the ex-SYJR line did not reach the pit until the following year. Work did not restart at Firbeck until 1923, and coal was produced two years later, with the SYJR-promoted 'light railway' being opened to full mineral standards by 1926. A connecting third side at Harworth Junction and the GNR/SYJR connection at the colliery were both opened by the LNER in 1929.

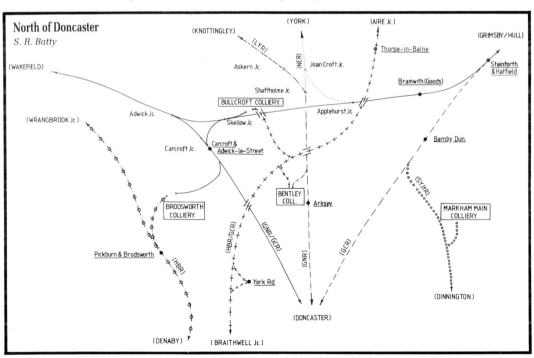

North of Doncaster
S. R. Batty

Coal Traffic and the St Leger

For most of the year these two features of life in Doncaster lived side by side with each other, continuing on along their own paths and not having any common effect on the town. By the turn of the century, the St Leger race week had developed to the point where all the town's railway goods and mineral traffic was halted for the full week in order to handle the influx of racegoers. In contrast the St Leger meetings of the 1990s come and go without making even the smallest ripple upon British Rail's daily operating procedures — in railway terms it is a non-event. However, 100 years ago the town and the meeting were reaping the full benefits of some 60 years of railway expansion and the development of cheap railway travel which had become available to thousands of people in an industrialised world. The railway arrangements necessary to handle the numbers of passengers who would arrive for a St Leger meeting of the later 1890s were enormous and, viewed against today's railway business, they defy belief.

Above left:
A coal train from the Harworth/Firbeck branch leaves Firbeck Junction towards Maltby behind Class O4/8 2-8-0 No 63738 on 23 July 1963. This branch is now lifted. *M. Mitchell*

Left:
Another 'O4/8', No 63785, approaches Harworth colliery along the now lifted GNR branch from the ECML with a train of empties on 15 April 1965. *A. Moyes*

Above:
Class 58 No 58027 prepares to leave Harworth Colliery on 27 March 1990. *S. R. Batty*

Right:
A horse ambulance built at the Plant for use at Doncaster racecourse and photographed in March 1920. *NRM (Don W4)*

During the entire race week, all sidings at the Plant, the carriage works and the yards all around the town were cleared of all wagons and rolling stock to make room for stabling excursion trains. The Plant and carriage works were closed down and no further coal or goods wagons were allowed into the town. Privately-owned coal wagons would be sent away to be parked up in any colliery siding or goods siding outside the area which could take them. In terms of racegoers, the St Leger was truly the GNR's own race meeting — about 70,000 could be expected to attend, and of these around 60,000 would have arrived at the company's Doncaster station on the day of the race. All available siding space had been commandeered to hold over 200 trains if required, and these would mostly arrive from stations within a radius of about 80 miles. If the GNR had not been able to handle these trains the meeting would have been a flop, but years of practice saw the week's activities honed to perfection. A 'Special and Additional' working timetable was printed, which typically contained 50 pages of closely-spaced print and was required reading for *everyone*. Nine signalboxes which normally closed after the evening shift were kept open as long as was required, and three temporary signalboxes were erected to provide extra block sections for further capacity. Extra signals were built, all sidings and approaches were operated on the absolute block system, and extra flagmen were sent out to supervise all level crossings and hand points and all shunting operations. On the great day itself about 160 trains would arrive and have to be stabled before returning during the afternoon and evening. No through goods traffic was allowed to use the station between 07.00 and 21.00, with only express fish traffic being allowed through. In addition, empty coaching stock movement was banned for a 24-hour period from 22.00 on the previous day, and all through carriage working was stopped from 10.00 prompt. Even the

regular traffic which normally passed non-stop through the station was made to halt during the busiest hours, so great was the activity in the area.

Every passenger on the excursion trains was given a notice with details of the return train's departure, including the *precise spot* where each carriage would be parked alongside the platform! Notices to identify each train were stuck on the locomotive, the carriage sides and even the end of the brakevan — one wonders how many revellers still managed to get it wrong, especially if they had enjoyed a lucky day on the Townmoor! The returning trains were all marshalled and ready to leave for the station by 13.30, some three hours before the first departure was scheduled to leave the station. Between 17.30 and 19.30 the specials were leaving at the rate of one per minute, and by 20.00 some 60,000 travellers had been despatched from the station.

When the week was over Doncaster station would resume its usual activities and the coal traffic would start to flow again, and someone, somewhere, would sit down and perhaps refine the plan just a little, here and there, to cater for next year's meeting. Doncaster station has never been more than a modest affair, and the Cherry Lane station (closed to passengers in 1852) was always pressed into use at these times. Running powers by this time extended to the NER, GER, GCR, LYR, LNWR and MR, with the GCR being the second largest user and the MR being the smallest. Companies were not allocated to specific platforms, and a typical weekday would see 152 trains depart and 136 arrive, with only 26 running non-stop. Goods traffic included no less than 330 trains *daily* being sent by the GNR alone; this figure makes the GCR total of 90 trains look paltry by comparison. The Great Eastern Railway were making full use of the GN/GE Joint line to the tune of 60 trains daily, whilst the LYR managed 18 per day and even the mighty London & North Western Railway conjured up some 14 daily goods

Above:

Every siding in the area was used for stabling the St Leger traffic. This Class B16/1 4-6-0 No 61456 leaving the Down Decoy yard with a train of mineral empties on 30 June 1958. The yard would not have been disrupted by the small amount of race rail traffic generated in the later 1950s.
P. J. Lynch

Below:

Class V2 2-6-2 No 60923 heads north from Doncaster on 31 July 1963. Another 'V2' is coupled ahead of a 'Baby Deltic' Type 2 diesel loco by the 'C' signalbox in the left background. *E. Treacy*

trains. (The LNWR's running powers to Doncaster dated back to 1879, when a GNR/LNWR joint line agreement was made concerning a rural branch in Leicestershire; part of the agreement gave the company access to Doncaster — and the coal traffic — via Retford, and the LNWR used these powers to run coal trains to London via this cross-country route between the East and West Coast main lines.) All this traffic was flowing in the years before the GCR's avoiding line was built and before the North Bridge improvements were carried out — the 19 signalboxes which controlled the station approaches would certainly have been fully utilised.

6: In Top Form, 1900-40

The Plant

Locomotive matters at the Plant changed from 1895, following Stirling's death and his replacement by Henry A. Ivatt, a Crewe-trained engineer who was recruited to the GNR from the Great Southern & Western Railway at Cork, Ireland. Stirling's locomotives had handled the express passenger traffic capably, and with many a demonstration of outstanding power output and speed ability, since the 1870s, but increasing loads were taking their toll by the 1890s. The Stirling locos could only manage when handled by expert crews who knew how to get the very best out of these machines — the express motive power fleet was having to be nursed along, and nothing was left in reserve. Ivatt's task was to renew the fleet, and two problems faced him. Firstly, both goods and passenger traffic was increasing rapidly, with the latter also being required to run at ever-faster schedules; and, secondly, the locomotive-building capacity of both the GNR and of private contractors was fully stretched, other railway companies being in similar positions and all the locomotive builders having full order books. The Plant's ability was directed towards producing mainly 0-6-0 goods locos with bigger boilers and cylinders, and small runs of 4-4-0 and even 2-4-0 and 4-2-2 passenger types.

Ivatt was a firm believer in good firebox and boiler design, and in 1898 Doncaster turned out his Atlantic 4-4-2 No 990, the first of this wheel arrangement in Great Britain (just beating the LYR product) and endowed with plenty of boiler capacity and firebox space. With a boiler which steamed effortlessly and sufficient adhesive weight to allow the tractive effort to be used in full at starting, No 990 was an instant success and clearly pointed the way ahead.

This locomotive was a development tool which Ivatt used before putting the 4-4-2 into series production at the Plant, which meanwhile was steadily turning out the new goods locos needed across the system. A total of 21 Atlantics (known as 'Klondykes', after the Alaskan gold rush of the time) was built by 1903, and the same boiler was used from 1901 on a series of 0-8-0 goods engines known as 'Long Toms', which could easily manage trains of over 700 tons from Peterborough to London.

Ivatt followed Sturrock's philosophy that the measure of a good locomotive was its capacity to boil water — a simple rule which summed up his boiler

designs for the Atlantics. The 'Klondykes' were performing well but he could see that even more power would soon be needed, and in 1902 his Large Atlantic, No 251, appeared to an astonished railway audience. Like the 'Klondykes' the tractive effort was no greater than that of the Stirling 8ft Singles, but the large-diameter boiler and new, wide firebox which was swept outwards over the trailing wheels gave No 251 a previously undreamt-of steam-raising ability. This is not to forget the ability also of the fireman who had to shovel the amount of fuel needed, but the efficiency of the new boilers was a revelation. A total of 83 such Atlantics was built between 1902 and 1910, and these machines went on to produce some tremendous feats of haulage and speed, especially in later, LNER, days. In the 1930s an Atlantic would often stand in for a failed Gresley Pacific and would keep or even regain time; the schedules of the streamlined trains were no deterrent to these remarkable steam-raisers.

As mentioned earlier, the Plant was fully occupied with loco repair and building work at the turn of the century. Ivatt secured an increase in new locomotive building from 35 to 45 per year from 1907, taking advantage of the new manufacturing techniques and power sources which had recently been introduced. While the Plant was turning out some excellent locomotives, the carriage works was replacing the GNR's coaching stock, some of which was just not good enough for the long hauls along the East Coast. In 1905 Herbert Nigel Gresley was appointed Carriage and Wagon Superintendent at the early age of 29 years. He immediately set about introducing many new ideas into the coaching fleet, such as using steel underframes, buckeye couplers, elliptical-section roofs, electric lighting and double-bolster bogies. These features gradually appeared on new stock built for the ECJS services, and the famous Gresley teak bodywork was first seen during these years. The greatest problem lay with the fleet of six- and eight-wheeled non-bogie stock, which apart from being real rough-riders, bucketing along and jarring over every rail-joint, were almost antediluvian in concept, lacking any feature which could be remotely concerned with passenger comfort. Gresley's predecessor, E.F. Howlden, had made great progress in building modern stock, but too many of the old non-bogie vehicles were still in service. These were improved by rebuilding into articulated sets of coaches, where two

Above:
The slender lines of Ivatt's 'Klondyke' 4-4-2s hid a powerful machine which took over the express duties from the older Stirling engines. Here No 988 hauls an up express at Greenwood about 1911, the immaculate and graceful locomotive contrasting sharply with the motley collection of rolling stock assembled behind the tender. *NRM (LDY/Box 21)*

Below:
The large-boilered development of the Atlantic theme was Ivatt's masterpiece. No 301, works No 1074 of May 1905, reposes at King's Cross loco. *NRM (749/79)*

bodies were permanently coupled together using three bogies to give a better ride which, when taken with the other various improvements made at the same time, resulted in a far better fleet of vehicles for the GNR's second-string services. Articulated sets of up to five bodies were built over the years to 1914, and these trains became a feature of GNR/LNER/BR(E) passenger services which did not finally disappear until the 1960s. They were perhaps most commonly seen on suburban workings around King's Cross, but the technique was sufficiently refined for special articulated sets to be built for the

Above:
ECJS twin corridor composite vehicles 202 and 206, formed in 1905 from a pair of six-wheelers dating from 1890. *NRM (Don 44A)*

Right:
The interior of three third-class dining saloons, Nos 313-315, built during 1900. *NRM (Don 396)*

Leeds service in 1921, for the 'Flying Scotsman' in 1928 and for the streamlined trains of the mid-1930s.

By the watershed year of 1914 the Plant was on the crest of a wave. It was producing ever-more powerful locomotives (especially after Gresley was promoted to Locomotive, Carriage & Wagon Superintendent in 1911) and the use of modern techniques had made the Crimpsall into a self-contained locomotive repair shop which was responsible for maintaining the entire fleet, instead of having much of the work done at the five main running sheds (King's Cross, Peterborough, Lincoln, Ardsley and Grantham) where standards and facilities could vary. The carriage works was producing rolling stock to match the quality of the motive power and the main line permanent way, with the west shop being enlarged in 1913 to enable more work to be handled. Then came the war. Munitions production and other work connected with the war effort took an ever-increasing share of the Plant's capacity from 1915 onwards, covering manufacturing of large ammunition, reconditioning of shell cases, making gun parts and mountings and building horse-drawn wagons. Part of the old tender shop was fitted out with lathes, presses, buffing machines and tapping machines, and the lower turnery was equipped with more lathes especially for 6in shell production. Some of the tools belonged to the GNR, but others were requisitioned from local factories. With the new tools came a new workforce too — as the Plant's staff were drawn into the fighting in France, the local women were recruited to do many of the new jobs being carried out in the works as well as some of the less arduous jobs amongst the regular railway tasks. Doncaster's women were to be seen producing shells large and small, operating all types of machine tools, and coping with all types of tasks at the stations, carriage & wagon depots, in the Plant and at Carr loco.

Some positive developments took place during these dark days, however, mostly connected with

Gresley's plans to produce a fleet of large and powerful locomotives which would be able to handle anything which the traffic department might demand in the years ahead. His large-boilered Class O1 2-8-0 freight locomotive had appeared in 1913 and was instantly successful, but Gresley was keen to exploit high boiler power by the use of three or four cylinders, and he then spent a considerable amount of time and effort in resolving the best layout to follow for his planned new fleet. Ivatt had laid the foundations of the excellent boiler designs which the GNR then had, and he had also advised Gresley never to use four cylinders if three would do the job. Gresley took this advice and set about the task of designing a drive gear for the middle cylinder which would be operated by the drives to the outside cylinders, so saving the complications of providing eccentrics and radius rods within the loco frames. His effort culminated in the building of 2-8-0 No 461 in May 1918 with three cylinders using a two-to-one rocking shaft arrangement which positively bristled with levers and pin joints which the technical press of the day was quick to point out would surely lead to wear problems within a relatively short time. A rather simpler arrangement had been patented in 1909 by H. Holcroft, one of Churchward's colleagues on the

GWR, and this gentleman quickly got in touch with Gresley after No 461 appeared. The resulting co-operation led to the design of a much simpler two-to-one lever arrangement which was a model of simplicity compared to the first valvegear drive design. Regardless of this, No 461 satisfied all Gresley's hopes for three-cylinder propulsion, and the stage was set for his future expansion scheme. In March 1920 Class K1 2-6-0 No 1000 appeared, fitted with the new valvegear and a massive boiler of 6ft diameter, and in 1922 came the first Pacific, No 1470 *Great Northern*. The rest, as they say, is history

The interwar years of 1918-39 saw none of the hectic activity which had characterised the pre-1914 era. Road traffic competition and the general trade depression led to lean times all round. Building the larger and heavier locomotives involved small improvements such as an increase in lifting capacity of cranes etc, but very little new construction was undertaken (especially with carriages and wagons) until conditions improved somewhat from the mid-1930s. By 1930 the old erecting shop and the tender shop were both converted into a new machine shop and the old upper and lower turneries were closed. A great saving was made in transport costs involved in moving components around the Plant, and the former upper turnery was converted into a drawing office. Both the engine and tender repair shops were reorganised several times to reflect the reduced needs of the LNER loco fleet. One bay of the tender shop was used for the repair of superheater flues and boiler tubes and the second bay was used for boiler repairs. Tender

Below:
Newly-assembled Class V1 2-6-2T No 461 seen inside the Plant during April 1936. *W. L. Good*

repairs were then carried out in two pits in one of the engine repair shop's original erecting bays, and the remaining pits were used for axlebox manufacture and repair. Engine repairs were confined to just two bays in the repair shop, whilst locomotives were stripped in the old tender shop. A new Weighing House was built in 1935 between the engine repair shop and the paint shop, and a central compressor station was built in 1936 using three compressors giving a capacity of 750cu ft/minute. The foundry was extended (although a large item, such as a 'Sandringham' three-cylinder one-piece casting, would still have to be produced by an outside supplier or another LNER foundry, such as Gorton) and oil furnaces were installed in the Flanging House. The Plant's electricity generating equipment was sold off after 1918 and a supply was taken directly from Doncaster corporation, but this agreement was terminated from 1922-1925 and replaced by arrangements made with the Doncaster Collieries Association. An 11,000-Volt supply was taken from the colliery supply network into a sub-station at Potteric Carr and then fed by cables both to the Plant and to Carr wagon works. Each location then used transformers and switchgear to distribute the power as required, and rotary converters were used to provide a direct-current supply where necessary.

The gloom lifted briefly during the last years before the outbreak of war in 1939 to give the LNER — and Doncaster — its finest years. From 1935 all the company's design work was concentrated at the Plant, and in the same year new services were introduced which called for locomotives and coaching stock of a type never before seen. The first of the streamlined 'A4' Pacifics, No 2509 *Silver Link*, emerged in September 1935 and went into service almost immediately with the 'Silver Jubilee', a 4hr Newcastle service which set unbelievable standards of speed and comfort for the times. Mile after mile was run at speeds of 85-90mph, and the specially-built seven-car articulated coach sets were soon running to full capacity. The original sets were made of two twin sets and one triplet set, but such was demand for the train that an extra body was added to one of the twin sets in the late 1930s. (The tare weight was increased from 220 to 248 tons.) *Silver Link* worked the service unassisted for the first two weeks without mishap before No 2510 *Quicksilver* appeared, followed shortly by Nos 2511 *Silver King* and 2512 *Silver Fox*. The train was withdrawn in September 1939, never to reappear, but it had run approximately 540,000 miles, all without failure, and produced an estimated revenue of 63p/mile for the LNER. Passengers were prepared to pay for high speed and high quality, and two more streamlined trains appeared in 1937. In July the 'Coronation' started running from King's Cross to Edinburgh on a 6hr schedule, using a nine-coach set of 312 tons tare weight and requiring the 'A4' locomotive to work through to Edinburgh. The last coach of the set was an observation vehicle with 'beaver tail' construction, built to mirror the locomotive's streamlined front and also to reduce tail-end air resistance. Five more Pacifics were built for the new train, Nos 4488 *Union of South Africa*, 4489

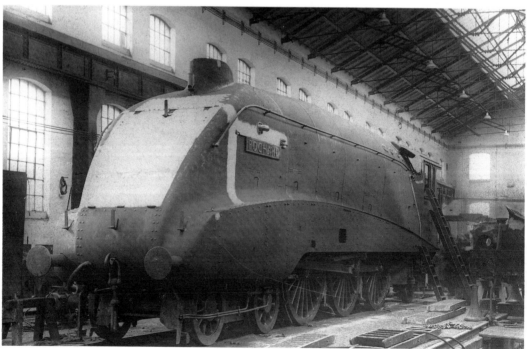

Below left:
Single-chimney 'A4' No 4499 *Pochard* **nears completion on 27 March 1938. The locomotive was renamed** *Sir Murrough Wilson* **in April 1939.** *W. L. Good*

Right:
Paint samples being exposed to the elements at the carriage works during early LNER days. *NRM (Don 37/47)*

Below:
'Coronation' observation cars under construction, on 10 May 1937. *NRM (Don 37/52)*

Dominion of Canada, 4490 *Empire of India,* 4491 *Commonwealth of Australia* and 4492 *Dominion of New Zealand.*

The last of the streamliners to appear was the 'West Riding Limited', which commenced in October 1937 using an eight-coach set to serve Leeds non-stop and then crawling over the 10 miles to Bradford Exchange. Leeds was reached in 2hr 43min and Bradford in 3hr 5min, the latter by courtesy of a pair of 'N2' 0-6-2T engines. Once again, 'A4' Pacifics were built for the new train — Nos 4495 *Golden Fleece* and 4496 *Golden Shuttle.* As with the 'Silver Jubilee', the last two streamliners disappeared for ever in 1939, but they had left yardsticks against which East Coast main line performances would be judged for many a year ahead.

War work returned in 1939, and the Plant turned out a mass of equipment both large and small. Perhaps the greatest difference compared with the World War 1 was the amount of 'pure' railway work that was required as part of the Plant's contribution. From 1942/43, American locomotives were being imported prior to the invasion of Europe (still a good two years off), and the LMS '8F' 2-8-0 was being built by vari-

us builders as a standard design to be used through-out the country (and ultimately in parts of Europe) as part of the war effort. The Plant modified some of the American locos for use at home, and Doncaster built the first of its batch of 30 LMS locos, No 8510, during May 1943. Construction of the LNER's own 'O2' class 2-8-0, which had ceased in 1934, was revived in 1942 and a further 25 built by January 1943. Curiously, the Plant's 1,942nd locomotive was one of this series, No 3844 (BR 63974) being delivered during November 1942.

The war work was not without its drama, too. Disaster struck the Plant on 21 December 1940 when the carriage building shop, carriage electricians' shop, chair shop and sawmill were all destroyed by fire. The flames attracted the attention of several enemy bombers in the area and a number of bombs were dropped in the Plant yard, but miraculously all failed

Left:
Steam galore in the Plant, 11 February 1962. *J. H. Turner*

Below left:
Two famous locomotives at the south end of Doncaster station. Class A3 No 60103 *Flying Scotsman* **heads for Kings Cross past Class A4 No 60017** *Silver Fox.* *J. H. Turner*

Below:
An assortment of motive power at Carr loco, on 5 April 1936. *J. S. Hancock*

to explode. Considerable damage was also caused to several carriages within the area, but fortunately no loss of life was reported. Carriage work was then greatly reduced until the shop was rebuilt during 1947-48, but the war years still saw some development take place when Thompson produced steel-panelled vehicles with an eye towards full-scale production after the war ended.

Motive Power Points

Even in the depressed years of the later 1920s, Carr loco had a workload of no mean proportions. Despite being placed rather less than half-way from King's Cross to Edinburgh, alongside the country's premier passenger-carrying railway, the shed's business was tied up entirely with the haulage of coal, meat, fruit and vegetables, and passenger turns were certainly not the prime business of the day. Perishable goods has to be moved fast, and by the summer of 1927 Carr loco had an allocation of 13 Pacific locomotives purely for such fast goods work. (Eight of these would run daily to London and back.) The eight goods yards in the area handled no less than 168,000 wagons per *month,* a task requiring 25 shunting locomotives and 75 sets of men daily. The depot was improved during the 1920s, principally with the building of a mechanical coaling plant (the 'Cenotaph') which could handle 3,500 tons of coal per week, a figure far beyond the capacity of the previous 'hand and tub' method. A sand-drier, wheel drop and

hot-water plant were added, together with a 65ft turntable at the south end of the layout. Each of the shed's 12 through roads had a preparation pit outside the building, and up to 18 locos could be placed over a disposal pit at any one time. These improvements no doubt eased the job of getting a locomotive on and off shed somewhat, but no steam loco depot was ever a clinically clean, ideally-equipped workplace. The amounts of ash to be shovelled into wagons, the frozen water columns in winter-time, the general lack of space and light in the shed building, and the endless shunting required, all would have combined to militate against good working conditions. It was not until 1938 that electric lighting was installed in the shed and yard, at the same time as the main shed building was re-roofed; presumably this was preceded by several years of pouring rainwater and howling gales! The immediate postwar years saw the building of oil storage tanks for use in the short-lived fuel-oil burning scheme, and by early 1948 two out of the planned four tanks were completed.

During the mid-1930s, the government-backed Assisted Loan Scheme allowed the LNER to build new locomotives (and stimulate employment), and to eliminate some of the older classes. Among the first to be earmarked for early withdrawal was the 'Klondyke' Atlantic class. In early 1936, No 3990 was working out her last days from Mexborough shed on the slow train services from Sheffield to Hull via Doncaster, before withdrawal in October 1937 and restoration to GNR livery for exhibition in York railway museum from January 1938. Of the 22 locomotives, only two received new numbers under a 1943 renumbering scheme, and even these had gone for scrap by the end of the war. Atlantic boilers were regularly used around the area for stationary steam-rais-

Left:
The former LNWR shed, June 1961.
P. C. H. Robinson

Below:
Carr signalbox, just south of the motive power depot, in October 1977. The remains of an earlier road access into the wagon works can be seen. *J. H. Turner*

Below right:
Two bridges across the Don — the LNER replacement for Rainbow Bridge, and the DVR Conisbrough viaduct in the background.
S. R. Batty

ng purposes, especially after withdrawal of the Ivatt Large Atlantics started in 1943. Quite often the full locomotive was parked up for use at the locomotive works, carriage shops or at Carr wagon shops, but sometimes just the boiler was retained and used around the Plant. Six such boilers lasted until 1965 before being condemned.

Locomotives from Mexborough shed were no strangers to Doncaster, working principally on the long hauls to Grimsby and Scunthorpe. Mexborough was a pure goods shed, with an allocation in 1923 of no less than 182 locos made up mostly of 0-8-0, 2-8-0 and 0-6-0 ('Pom-Pom') types. Water quality was always a problem as the borehole supply contained high levels of dissolved solids which not even a Kennicott softening plant could eliminate. A small sub-shed was located at Hexthorpe yard, but this was quickly closed by the LNER and used as a signing-on point thereafter. An even smaller, one-loco shed at Denaby was also demolished in 1923, but the former LNWR depot in Doncaster survived as a loco shed until the 1930s. Half of the building was used by G. & A. Bell, a firm of railway wagon repairers, and the other half had been used as a shed by the GER until the Grouping. Railway use died out, and Bell's took over the entire building by 1938.

Local Developments

One of the area's earliest pieces of railway civil engineering was altered drastically in 1928. The South Yorkshire Railway's line from Swinton crossed the Don at a point roughly midway between Cadeby and Warmsworth, on opposite banks of the river, by a structure known as the Rainbow bridge. The original

single-track bridge had been widened to double-track, but this was on its last legs by the 1920s. The three cast iron curved spans carried the tracks for 108ft at a height of 27ft above water level, and these were replaced by a simple girder bridge which was installed in two halves, laying one line at a time during two possessions of the track. The original version must have been a far greater visual attraction than the totally anonymous LNER replacement which is still in use today, carrying a relatively large amount of traffic both light and heavy.

Industrial development had taken place along the bank of the river towards Thorne, and in 1930 the LNER opened a two-mile branch line from Marshgate Junction to Wheatley Park goods depot, passing close by the site of the Strawberry Island coal wharf of the 1850s. An extension of about one mile was added in 1938 to reach Long Sandall, where the branch ended between the fork of the South Yorkshire Joint Line and the Doncaster-Thorne line. More construction took place during August 1937 when new road bridges were installed at the entrance to Marshgate (GC) goods yard, using girders which had been stored in the yard since being removed from a former crossing of the main line south of Carr loco during 1929. This work was part of the first stage of a rebuilding plan for the station area which was well under way by early 1938. During that summer the passenger subway was dug out during weekend engineering possessions of the down and up platform and through roads in turn. Not all went smoothly — during installation of the first subway girder below the down platform on 12 June, the girder jammed and the crane tipped badly, needing an extra 18 hours' work to rectify. A temporary facing crossover was installed — part of

the St Leger equipment — to allow wrong-line running during the work, and a 15mph speed limit was imposed on all traffic. Carr loco's 45-ton breakdown crane was used on all the weekends as required.

By the spring of 1939 the new up platform road was well under way, making the former platform into an island arrangement, and the northern end of the station layout had been altered greatly. The bottleneck remained, but it was to be removed very shortly by a widening scheme which would finally see off the congestion caused between Marshgate and Frenchgate Junctions, simply by rebuilding some existing sidings into full running lines. The passenger footbridge was taken out of use when the subway was finished in 1940, and a start was made on installing electrical signalling equipment, before the war stopped all work. It was to be 1949 before the widening and resignalling works were completed.

Right:
Invasion notice, 1940. *T. S. Walker*

Left:
Class 37 No 37218 shunts sand wagons at Kirk Sandall on 3 December 1990. This branch is now just a short connection from Kirk Sandall Junction, the original branch from Marshgate having closed in 1971. *S. R. Batty*

Below left:
Marshgate Junction in 1949, before remodelling. *C. T. Goode*

Below:
Marshgate Junction signalbox, photographed on 2 June 1979. *P. C. H. Robinson*

THE RAILWAY EXECUTIVE COMMITTEE

NOTICE
TO STAFF OF THE UNDERTAKINGS CONTROLLED BY THE MINISTER OF WAR TRANSPORT

Duty of Staff in the Event of Invasion

A Government leaflet headed "Beating the Invader" which has been delivered to every house advised everybody what to do in the event of invasion.

People were advised that—

(1) If they are in areas some way from the fighting they should stay in their own district and carry on as usual.

(2) If fighting breaks out in their neighbourhood and they are at work or have special orders they should carry on as long as possible and only take cover when danger approaches. If on their way to work they should finish the journey if possible.

In the case of staff of the Undertakings controlled by The Minister of War Transport, the following directions are in the nature of "special orders" as referred to in Clause (2) above.

In the event of invasion heavy responsibilities will fall upon the controlled Undertakings and it is imperative that all staff should be at their posts. You should, therefore, make every endeavour to continue to come to work, and if on any occasion you are unable to report for duty at the proper time you should do so at the earliest possible moment.

If invasion comes it will be defeated by calm courage and resolute action and it is confidently expected that all members of the staff will play their part.

7: Modern Times, 1948-91

Local Services

Whereas many parts of the railway system suffered drastic pruning measures during the 10 years after 1945, the Doncaster area escaped relatively unscathed. Some lines, of course, never got off the ground as far as passenger services were concerned; the H&BR's stations at Pickburn & Brodsworth, Sprotborough, and Denaby & Conisbrough all closed their doors to passengers in February 1903, and the H&BR/GCR joint Aire Junction-Braithwell Junction line never sold a single passenger ticket at all during its brief existence. The Hull & Barnsley Railway was taken over by the North Eastern Railway — the very company whose monopoly of the Hull coal traffic led to the formation of the H&BR — during 1922, and all passenger traffic between Hull and Cudworth was dispensed with from 1 January 1932. The passenger services along the Wath branch had already disappeared during April 1929, thus leaving the ex-H&BR system as nothing more than a basic mineral railway less than 50 years after the opening of the company's main line. The coal traffic decayed away in piecemeal fashion over the decades, with eventual closure often following a long period of disuse. On the Hull & South Yorkshire Extension Railway the Wath-Hickleton section fell into disuse after 1945, but formal closure to Moorhouse & South Elmsall did not take place until 31 May 1954, with the last section to Wrang-

brook going on 30 September 1963. All coal traffic from Hull to Wrangbrook stopped running from 29 November 1958, with official closure taking place from 6 April 1959. The last part of the H&BR main line, from Wrangbrook to Cudworth, closed as late as 7 August 1967, when the Denaby branch was also taken out of use.

After the closure of the Hull line in 1958, coal traffic from the remains of the two branches continued to be worked to Cudworth via a reversal at Wrangbrook, and, after final closure of the ex-H&BR lines the collieries involved simply used their existing alternative connections to previously-competing companies. Goods handling at the stations along the way must have been minimal, but the facilities remained available until, or just before, closure. Despite losing passenger traffic in 1903, the goods traffic handling lasted (at least on paper) at Pickburn & Brodsworth until 30 September 1963 and at Sprotborough until 10 August 1964; by some quirk of fate, the goods traffic at Denaby & Conisbrough had been halted from July 1927. Facilities on the Wath branch and along the Cudworth line remained until closure of the lines.

Of all local closures in the area, the H&BR/GCR joint line suffered the slowest death. The southern section from Warmsworth to Braithwell Junction was abandoned during World War 2 and the tracks used for storage of crippled wagons, but official closure

did not take place until 13 March 1969, by which time the sleepers had rotted, large trees had grown and the entire formation was almost fully reclaimed by nature — a real case of arboreous dereliction. The northern section closed on 20 October 1958 (ie almost at the same time as the H&BR main line) between Aire Junction and Bullcroft Junction, taking with it the goods facilities — assuming they had ever been used — at Pollington, Sykehouse and Thorpe-in-Balne. (The first station was renamed from Snaith & Pollington in July 1951, presumably to avoid confusion with Snaith station on the nearby Wakefield-Goole line.) In 1961, a short length was reopened from Bullcroft Junction to give access to the new Thorpe Marsh power station, but this was closed

from September 1970 when the present connection was laid in from the ex-WRGR line. At the same time the Bullcroft Junction-Doncaster (York Road) section was closed officially, the south curve at the station here having been abandoned in 1939. The short length between Sprotborough Junction (where the Joint line met the GCR's Doncaster avoiding line) and Warmsworth was closed officially from 3 February 1969, and the cutting beneath the Hexthorpe Junction lines was then filled in over the following years.

As already mentioned, the line never saw a regular passenger service at all, but at least one and possibly two trains did use the line to reach Doncaster. Unconfirmed reports speak of an H&BR Hull-Doncaster (York Road) race special being run during 1919

Below left:
Class 58 No 58019 *Shirebrook Colliery* near the site of Maltby station with empty mgr wagons on 27 March 1990. *S. R. Batty*

Right:
The derelict signalbox at the H&BR/GCR Aire Junction, photographed on 3 May 1953. *T. S. Walker*

Below:
A Leeds-King's Cross train approaches Hampole behind double-chimney 'V2' No 60902 on 23 April 1962. *P. Cookson*

A two-car DMU forming the 09.38 Doncaster-Sleaford passes through the closed station at Finningley on 16 July 1990.
S. R. Batty

Above:
Class J39 0-6-0 No 64825 passes South Elmsall with a down coal train on 20 May 1958. *P. Cookson*

Right:
The disused northern end of the DVR: buffer stops near Shafton, September 1990. *S. R. Batty*

via the direct route from Aire Junction instead of the more usual (and lengthier) run via Knottingley and Shaftholme Junction. The train which certainly did run was a two-car diesel multiple unit forming the RCTS 'Doncaster Decoy' railtour of 5 October 1968, which traversed the joint line, amongst others, before it was too late. Bullcroft colliery had been closed in 1968, but the rusting connection to the yard was still intact, and the line into Bentley colliery, still very much in production, was noted to be out of use. The section from here to Doncaster Junction, where the spurs into York Road station were laid, was very rusty due to the reduction in the amount of coal being taken by the H&BR/GCR route towards Thorpe Marsh Power Station.

The first postwar passenger station closure took place at Askern, on the ex-LYR Knottingley line, when services were temporarily withdrawn from 10 March 1947 and then permanently from 27 September of the following year. Goods handling survived for many years afterwards, finally disappearing on 5

October 1964 amidst a sudden rash of such withdrawals following the publication of the Beeching Report in 1963. Hampole, on the ex-WRGR Wakefield-Leeds Line, closed completely from 7 January 1952 and Arksey — the famous Stockbridge station of 1848, renamed in 1850 — surpassed its centenary before closure to passengers on 5 August 1952; the goods traffic survived a further 12 years to December 1964. Further north along the main line, passenger and goods traffic ended at Moss from 8 June 1953 and from Balne and Heck on 15 September 1958, goods traffic lasting until 6 July 1964 and 23 April 1963 respectively. The autumn of 1958 was a bad time for these small ECML stations in the locality; services ended at Rossington and Bawtry from 6 October of that year, goods traffic ending on 27 May 1963 and 30 April 1971 — a late date — respectively.

Until 1950 the railmotor passenger service operated along the Dearne Valley Railway survived in its original form, and then lasted until 10 September 1951 in the shape of an Ivatt 2-6-2T locomotive from

Wakefield shed hauling a single coach in push-pull fashion.The last two railmotors in use were Nos 50650 and 50656, and the push-pull fitted Ivatt tanks used in the last months were Nos 41283 and 41284, delivered to the shed when almost brand-new. Considering the rapid demise of many other passenger services on similar mineral lines, it is amazing the DVR trains survived so long; its longevity becomes almost miraculous when the half-hearted attitudes of the LYR/LMSR and the bare facilities provided for passengers are considered.The service never operated into Doncaster, and the somewhat remote terminus at Edlington ensured that prospective passengers looking for an easy route into the town would simply use road transport to reach either Doncaster or Barnsley. Wakefield was the centre of the DVR's passenger activity and people did actually use the service from the mining villages, despite the fares being relatively high compared to those charged via Doncaster and the ex-WRGR route; local bus transport also provided plenty of opposition on this route too. Despite the passengers being counted by the conductor/guard on the fingers of one hand for many years, the frequency of service remained much as had been provided during the 1920s; the closure in 1951 saw the end of three daily trips to Edlington and two to Goldthorpe only (both with one extra trip on Saturdays), and a return service of two trains all week from Edlington and two from Goldthorpe only, plus the extra Saturday train.

After losing the passenger service the ex-DVR line continued to serve the collieries for a further 15 years before any more change took place. Millions of tons of coal were taken out of the valley, mostly towards Wakefield and hauled almost exclusively by 'WD' class 2-8-0s which clanked and plodded their weary ways at speeds of around 15-20mph. Eventually, the coal seams which had made the DVR into a worthwhile mineral railway brought about its end. Subsidence at Conisbrough tunnel and viaduct took its toll, and a triangular junction was laid in at Houghton to connect the DVR (via a north-facing connection) onto the Midland main line during 1966. Closure from Grimethorpe to Goldthorpe took place from 11 July, coal from these collieries then using the new layout to reach Healey Mills via Cudworth and Royston.The northern end of the system, at Crofton Junctions, was also closed, and all remaining DVR signalling was controlled from the MR main line signalbox at Cudworth. Traffic from Yorkshire Main colliery continued to run to Black Carr West until 1972, when the ex-DVR connections to the GN/GE Joint line and the ECML were closed and traffic confined to the 1908 LYR spur onto the South Yorkshire Joint Line at St Catherine's.

On the GN/GE Joint line, Finningley station closed to passengers (despite a large RAF establishment nearby) from 11 September 1961. Park Drain, the next station towards Gainsborough, had closed in February 1955 after a rather under-used life of almost 60 years. The station had been opened in 1896 in the hope of catching trade from a planned coalfield development, but this did not materialise and the station remained, with the adjacent Park Drain Hotel, as a lonely outpost amidst the flat, fertile countryside. Goods handling remained at these two stations until 6 September 1965 and 6 April 1964 respectively.

At St James' Bridge station (Cherry Lane), dismantling was started during the summer of 1955, although the station was not taken out of use completely until June 1967, when the remaining goods traffic was dispensed with. The station's only passenger traffic was dealt with during race meetings, and this was falling away rapidly. After this was transferred to the main-line station, St James' quietly decayed away before complete demolition followed in the 1970s. By the mid-1960s the rail-borne St Leger traffic had disappeared completely. Re-roofing work at the station during the summer of 1957 saw the removal of the cast-iron colonnades which had supported the structures since 1877, in an exercise which included the renewal of the roofing above platform 4.

The last round of passenger station closures took place in 1967, when two of the ex-West Riding & Grimsby stations were closed. Barnby Dun finished handling passengers on 4 September, and Carcroft & Adwick-le-Street followed on 6 November, when the Leeds stopping service was withdrawn. Goods traffic had disappeared from both stations in 1965, on 5 April and 28 June respectively. Carcroft station must have been a signwriter's dream; opening in 1866 as plain Adwick, it was re-named Adwick-le-Street & Carcroft in March 1867 and re-named again in May 1880 to become Carcroft & Adwick-le-Street.

Goods and mineral lines featured in the last round of closures of station facilities in the area when the South Yorkshire Joint Line, bereft of passengers since 1929, lost its goods handling facilities by 1965; those at far-off Anston had gone in December 1950, but traffic handling lasted at Tickhill & Wadworth (Tickhill until July 1911) until 2 November 1964, at Dinnington & Laughton until 3 May 1965 and at Maltby until 14 June 1965. The ex-GCR goods yard at Marshgate closed from 30 April 1971, followed by the Wheatley Park/Kirk Sandall branch in August of the same year.

Plant Matters

Steam locomotive development was brought to a halt during the war years, but the LNER soon started making plans for construction of a standard series of express passenger locomotives for use after the hostilities ended. Sir Nigel Gresley played a leading role during the prewar years in bringing British locomotive boiler design very close to its peak of development, leaving only the improvement of front-end draughting arrangements as an area where any future significant changes could be made. He was certainly aware of the benefits to be had from using the Kylchap double blast-pipe and chimney arrangement — two 'A4s', Nos 4468 *Mallard* and 4901 *Capercaillie,* were so equipped from new — and any future designs from 1938 would certainly have made use of them, but his early death in 1941 saw the end of a famous line of locomotive development. The war effort saw a drastic cut in maintenance standards and the haulage of terrific loads which were far beyond any limits ever envisaged for the locomotive fleet. Inevitably, the strain took its toll and failures occurred, but the three-cylinder fleet soldiered on

and kept the LNER's express passenger and goods traffic moving.

Gresley was succeeded in his post by Edward Thompson, who immediately set about producing locomotives to form a basis for the postwar years, but who also seemed determined to undo much of Gresley's good work in locomotive design over the previous 25 years. Between 1943 and 1945 he produced a series of locomotives by rebuilding various Gresley machines to test his ideas for the future, and unfortunately all seemed to have been built as much to spite his predecessor as to produce any worthwhile improvement in locomotive design. His intentions of designing locomotives which would require less

Right:
Two views inside the Plant during April 1936. The first shows the boiler and frames of Class P2 2-8-2 No 2003 Lord President being built up, with the double blastpipe assembly on the shop floor and the two-to-one lever ready for fitting.
W. L. Good

Below:
The second scene shows the frames of another 'P2', probably No 2004 Mons Meg, being assembled.
W. L. Good

maintenance and which would be just as versatile and powerful as Gresley's machines produced only a very few useful pointers to the future. Most of his work was concentrated on the various 'A2' sub-classes, and it was not until May 1946 that a series of 15 Class A2/3 Pacifics was put into production at Doncaster. These were regarded as the best of his locomotives, but they did not have the sheer power of Gresley's machines. Thompson's first locos to be turned out of the Plant were six Class A2/2 rebuilds of Gresley's Class P2 2-8-2 locomotives which had done excellent work between Edinburgh and Aberdeen since 1934; the rebuilds were despatched northwards from January 1943, only to be shunned by the Scottish crews as virtually useless compared to their previous incarnation. The four Class A2/1 machines built at Darlington from May 1944 were essentially a Pacific version of the superb 'V2' 2-6-2, but turned out to be somewhat under-boilered and led a quiet life until their final withdrawal during 1960/61.

Thompson's greatest folly was reserved for No 4470 *Great Northern* herself, which emerged in rebuilt Class A1/1 form in August 1945 to the disbelief of the railway world. The elegant lines of the pioneer GNR 4-6-2 had been completely destroyed, not only by the Thompson arrangement of long smokebox and cylinders placed to the rear of the bogie, but also by extending the running plate back at a high level and so cutting short the cab sheets. Certain people in authority tried to persuade Thompson not to rebuild No 4470, which carried so much GNR kudos, in such a vicious way, but all failed. As a prototype for future designs the rebuilt No 4470 was a failure, but the culmination of Thompson's 4-6-2 work, the Class A2/3, was a reasonable locomotive. To be fair to their design, the 'A2' variants included some good points which were carried over into BR designs. Rocking firegrates and ashpans made engine disposal simpler, the use of three sets of valvegear made maintenance easier in an era when skilled labour was hard to find, and the use of a good Kylchap design of front end meant that many of the locos were very free-running at speed. Until the Gresley machines were rejuvenated by the fitting of this feature during the 1950s, No 4470 (60113 in BR days) was known as a particularly good steamer by comparison with a single-chimney 'A3' or 'A4'. The Thompson rebuilds suffered mainly from poor adhesion factors, causing heavy slipping when starting, and problems with frames and axleboxes caused mainly by the large amount of surgery carried out to the front ends during rebuilding. Again, to be fair, the war effort would not have allowed the luxury of producing new components — frames, cylinders, motions, boilers — and Thompson would have had to do his best with whatever material was available. The authorities at the Ministry of Supply would not have allowed raw materials to be used for construction of new, prototype express passenger

locomotives in 1942/43 when the war was at its height and the running of express passenger trains was the last thing on anyone's mind; the need was for straightforward, rugged locos which could be almost mass-produced and used for haulage of freight, especially fuel and munitions. Thompson met this need on the LNER with the 'B1' 4-6-0, which, together with Gresley's 'V2' 2-6-2, was produced during the war years and gave sterling service across the entire system. The 'B1' was Thompson's best product, lasting almost to the end of steam traction on BR, but none were built at Doncaster. Edward Thompson was succeeded as Chief Mechanical Engineer in the summer of 1946 by Arthur Henry Peppercorn, very much a pro-Gresley man. His first act was to end the run of 'A2/3' Pacifics being built at the Plant and substitute his own refined version, known simply as Class A2. Divided drive and three sets of valvegear were retained, as was the rocking firegrate and ashpan, but the cylinders were moved forward to their usual place above the bogie, and the boiler dome, cab front and chimney were all revised to give a better, more elegant appearance. Only one loco was built with a Kylchap exhaust arrangement — surely a backward step, perhaps done in a hurry to regain the Gresley appearance? — but four were rebuilt from the single-chimney form in 1949. They were capable, well-liked locomotives which lasted well into the 1960s but never had a reputation for free running. Peppercorn's best design during his brief reign at Doncaster was his Class A1 4-6-2, essentially a 6ft 8in version of the 'A2' with Kylchap exhaust which appeared in August 1948, eight months after nationalisation. A total of 48 locomotives was built, 26 at Doncaster and 22 at Darlington, and all were in service by the end of 1949. These were good locomotives with a reputation for free running — especially the five locos, Nos. 60153-7, fitted with roller bearings to all axleboxes — but were always rather heavier on coal than a Gresley Pacific.

After 1948 the Plant was involved in the design and production of the new BR Standard class locomotives. Design work was concentrated on cylinders, valvegear, coupling and connecting rods. Building work started in 1950 with a batch of 50 LMS-designed Class 4 2-6-0 'Flying Pigs', a series which BR decided to continue until the new standard product was available. A run of 10 Class 4 2-6-4T locos was built in 1954, 42 Class 5 4-6-0s were built from 1951 and no less than 70 Class 4 2-6-0 tender locos — the BR version of the LMS product — were built between 1952 and 1957. The last of this series, No 76114, was turned out of the Plant on 14 October 1957 and marked the end of steam locomotive construction at the Plant. The erecting shop had been turned over to new locomotive building only during the building of the 'A1' Pacifics in 1948, and this event marked the beginning of 10 hectic years of locomotive work. No 76114 was the 2,228th loco to

be built at the Plant; the first had been 0-4-2 No 18, built in 1867.

The works numbers issued over the 90-year period give an insight into GNR/LNER locomotive development. No 50 was 4-2-2 No 1, built in 1870; No 500 was an 0-4-4T loco built for the London surburban services in 1890, one of 711 Stirling locomotives built at the Plant; No 1000 was 'Klondyke' Atlantic No 254 built in 1903 and one of Ivatt's 638 locomotives; the last of Gresley's 560 locos was Class V4 2-6-2 No 3402, works No 1920 of 1941, and the 2,000th locomotive was 'A2/3' No 500, completed in May 1946. Due to the strong LMS influence in the new British Railways management structure, many thought that all future locomotive building from 1950 onwards would be done at Crewe and that 'A1' No 60162 could well be the last product to appear from the Plant; fortunately the LMS workshop capacity was not great enough to produce all the new locos deemed necessary and keep the existing fleet running too.

Diesel locomotive building started in earnest during 1957 with a series of 204hp and 350hp shunting locomotives (a handful of diesel-electric shunters had been built in 1944), and the Plant began building electric locos from 1959 when a series of 24 750 Volt DC locomotives was started for the Southern Region's Kent Coast electrification scheme. The frames for the last of this order were laid during the spring of 1960, by which time preliminary work had started on a

Above:
A diesel shunter being assembled on 3 December 1943, showing the frames and the English Electric power unit in the background. These locos were numbered No 15000-003 in BR days. *NRM (Don 43/130)*

Above right:
Peppercorn Class A2 No 60533 *Happy Knight* **reposes in Doncaster mpd during December 1949 after having received a double chimney and green paintwork during a visit to the Plant.** *T. G. Hepburn*

Right:
A 'before and after' scene at Carr loco in April 1958. Class A3 No 60045 *Lemberg* **awaits entry to the Plant for repairs, whilst Class A1 No 60132** *Marmion*, **freshly despatched from the paint shop, awaits a turn of duty.** *J. H. Turner*

series of 25kV AC locos for the West Coast electrification project. Construction started during the summer of 1962, the 40 machines being known in later years as Class 85, and a further batch of 40 (Class 86) locos was built during 1965/66.

The End of Steam

The rundown of the BR steam fleet was dictated by, amongst other factors, the rate at which reliable diesel power was made available to displace the existing steam locomotives. Many virtually brand-

Top:
Class 'WD' 2-8-0 No 90044 at Carr loco on 17 June 1951.
R. E. Vincent

Above:
Ex-works 'K3' 2-6-0 No 61940 moves along the shed yard on 9 April 1960. *J. H. Turner*

Top right:
Carr loco yard in 1963, with plenty of Gresley motive power in evidence. *J. H. Turner*

Centre right:
The 'Plant line' is towed through the station on 31 May 1957. Class O2 2-8-0 No 63969 is hauling 'K3' No 61834, 'A1' Pacifics Nos 60146 *Peregrine* and 60113 *Great Northern*, and '4MT' 2-6-0 No 43130. *P. J. Lynch*

Right:
Class 9F 2-10-0 No 92142 crosses the Don at Doncaster North Junction with a York-bound goods on 24 August 1963. *A. W. Martin*

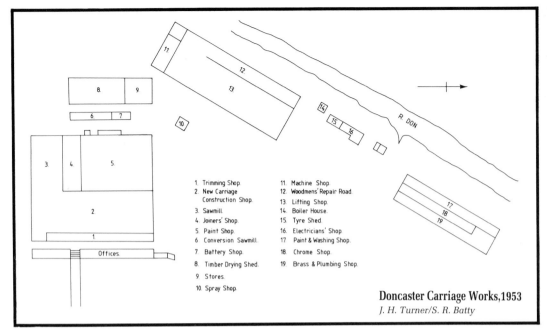

1. Trimming Shop.
2. New Carriage Construction Shop.
3. Sawmill.
4. Joiners' Shop.
5. Paint Shop.
6. Conversion Sawmill.
7. Battery Shop.
8. Timber Drying Shed.
9. Stores.
10. Spray Shop.
11. Machine Shop.
12. Woodmens' Repair Road.
13. Lifting Shop.
14. Boiler House.
15. Tyre Shed.
16. Electricians' Shop.
17. Paint & Washing Shop.
18. Chrome Shop.
19. Brass & Plumbing Shop.

Doncaster Carriage Works, 1953
J. H. Turner/S. R. Batty

new locos were condemned to an early scrapping, as well as many more which had years of mechanical toil left within their frames. The East Coast main line was a top-earner for BR and was thus destined for early dieselisation, thereby sending hundreds of steam locomotives to the scrapyard.

The dieselisation programme was to apply to all classes of traffic, and therefore all classes of locomotive would rapidly be affected. Diesels of Classes 31 and 40 arrived during the late 1950s and the imminent arrival of the 3,300hp 'Deltics' posed the first threats for ER steam; classes with a doubtful future by late 1959 were the 'A2' and 'A3' 4-6-2s, the 'V2' 2-6-2s, 'O2' and 'WD' 2-8-0s and 'L1' 2-6-4Ts. However, the early predictions often proved to be a little rash, for in early 1960 at the same time as four ER Class WD 2-8-0s were condemned, no less than 1,007 large locomotives were chosen for fitting with speedometers in view of their expected longer life span, and this included 16 'A4s', 26 'A3s', 6 'A2s', 10 'A1s', 8 'V2s' and 19 'Britannia' Pacifics!

Scrapping operations at the Plant included various ex-LMSR locos at the rate of about four per week, and the entire 'Sandringham' and 'Footballer' classes were eliminated after the dieselisation of East Anglia. This latter development resulted in the general appearance of 'Britannia' Pacifics at Doncaster after several were transferred from Norwich to Immingham in late 1960, beginning with Nos 70039-41. Standard Class 5 and 'Britannia' locomotives were overhauled at the Plant, including those allocated to the Western Region; indeed, Nos 73023 and 73068 arrived in black livery during 1960 and left the works in July resplendent in GWR-style green! (This was not Don-

caster's only gesture towards Swindon practice; in 1952, 'V2' No 60854 had been modified in accordance with current Swindon blastpipe/chimney practice and was despatched from the Plant with a copper-capped chimney. It ran in this form from October to December, when it was seen by Authority at King's Cross and rapid removal was ordered!)

The summer of 1961 was the last for steam haulage on the non-stop London-Edinburgh turn, a decision which coincided with the realisation of some of the best performances of the ex-LNER Pacifics in terms of utilisation and reliability. Work done during the 1950s to improve front-end performance and lubrication of the middle big-end bearings was paying handsome dividends; the roller-bearing 'A1s' had accumulated almost five million miles in 12 years and could manage 120,000 miles between shoppings, well above even the improved Gresley Pacifics. The Class 40 diesels appeared on Newcastle and through Edinburgh workings during 1960, and the first 'Deltic', No D9001, started test running during March 1961.

Dieselisation took rather longer to achieve than at first expected. During an 11hr period on 12 August 1961 a total of 121 locomotives was observed of which only 17 were diesel; the steam contingent included 30 'B1', 20 'A1', 12 'K3', 11 'V2', 10 'A2' and seven 'A4', the latter principally on Leeds duties. Problems with the 'Deltics' in particular, and train-heating boilers in general, overtook BR's intentions, and steam power was often on top-class turns such as the 'Flying Scotsman' and the 'Talisman'. Slight changes were made at the Plant to reflect the new conditions. The Crimpsall shop was partly given over to 'Deltic' overhaul work, and steam loco overhauls continued for the time being. From late 1961, all 'V2' locos were sent to Doncaster for shopping, but the first five from the ER/NER fleet were withdrawn during early 1962. Similarly all work on 'O1' class 2-8-0s was concentrated on the Plant, in preparation for the closure of Gorton works in Manchester. Nevertheless the great freeze of early 1962 saw 20 'A3' locos reprieved in the face of ever-mounting diesel casualties, and the King's Cross fleet of 'A1s' and 'A4s' was particularly evident on the Leeds services. When the weather improved the Leeds 'Peak' class diesels appeared on the West Riding expresses, followed 12 months later by the first members of Class 47. Steam haulage out of King's Cross ended officially in June 1963, and in August BR announced that no further general repairs would be carried out on the steam fleet. The end of steam work at the Plant came in November, when the last two steam locomotives were outshopped — 'WD' 2-8-0 No 90153 and 'A4' 4-6-2 No 60009 *Union of South Africa*.

Steam servicing continued for the time being at Carr loco, the shed becoming something of a dumping ground for stock from other closed depots in the area. Diesel power arrived, and had to be serviced as well as could be managed in the old steam shed. Class 47 locos appeared on the Thorpe Marsh merry-go-round during February 1964, displacing the usual 'WD' 2-8-0 power, and trials started for the West Burton service during summer 1965. Plenty of steam power was evident on local freight workings, though, and on several passenger turns, too. Ex-GCR and LNER 2-8-0 and 'WD' 2-8-0 types remained plentiful during 1964, and the 'B1' 4-6-0s still had booked passenger duties to Leeds and Hull. 'V2' 2-6-2s ran throughout the year, particularly towards York and along the GN/GE Joint line towards March. When Mexborough shed closed in March 1964, all duties were transferred to Wath diesel depot, but Carr loco received redundant locomotives from Canklow, Retford and Staveley during June 1965. The BR Standard Class 9F 2-10-0 was well represented at the shed, and it was a great pity that these excellent machines, with their strong haulage ability and free-running high speed capacity, did not enjoy a longer reign on the GN main line. The fast, heavy freight traffic hauled between King's Cross, Peterborough, March and Doncaster had always demanded the use of powerful locomotives, and a brief period in 1952 had even seen the use of the WD 2-10-0 on these duties until the new '9F' design could be produced. The first of the class had arrived in September 1955, when No 92037 was used for clearance tests, and by early 1956 Nos 92067-76 had been allocated for working to

Below:
A beautiful scene of an 'A4' in her last days. No 60003 *Andrew K. McCosh* **leaves the station with the 13.27 departure for King's Cross on 6 January 1962.** *J. H. Turner*

Whitemoor yard. Their reign was destined to be a short one.

Doncaster station steam pilot disappeared during May 1964, and the 'B1' workings to Hull and Cleethorpes saw the end of the summer timetable. Visiting steam traction was a regular feature throughout 1965, including '9F' 2-10-0s, 'Britannia' Pacifics, 'B' 4-6-0s, ex-LMS 2-6-4Ts, and 'V2' 2-6-2s, but the number of locos arriving from the North Eastern Region, particularly York — fell drastically by the end of the year. Plans were announced during the summer to convert the steam shed into a dead-ended

diesel depot by the end of the year, by which time the steam allocation would have been dispensed with. By New Year 1966, only eight serviceable locomotives were allocated, and the mass withdrawals at the end of the winter timetable period left the entire Eastern Region without any serviceable locomotives at all. Carr loco lost its steam allocation from 18 April 1966, and only the barest minimum of facilities was left to service the occasional locomotive running down from Leeds or York — not even a tenderful of coal could be provided, and the locos were despatched back as quickly as possible. The York locos petered out dur-

Left:
The remains of 'A3' No 60058 *Blair Athol* being disposed of at the Plant in 1963. *J. H. Turner*

Below:
Of all the Gresley 'A4' Pacifics, No 60014 *Silver Link* was surely the most deserving of preservation. This famous locomotive is seen being scrapped at the Plant on 21 September 1963. *P. Gerald*

Below right:
An eastbound coal train heads through Thorne South on 17 April 1961. *P. Cookson*

ing the summer, and only a Holbeck 'Jubilee' 4-6-0 occasionally turned up for a night parcels working back to Leeds.

Thus the only steam locomotives at the shed were 47 cold machines awaiting disposal, and later in the year the depot was rebuilt to provide diesel servicing facilities. Diesel depots were also provided at three other locations in the Doncaster division, at Frodingham, Colwick and Immingham, with the locomotives being allocated primarily to the latter depot. This arose because of the great importance to BR of the large tonnage of traffic which flowed along the route to and from Scunthorpe and Immingham from the west; originating and terminating traffic within the division on this route was far greater than that on the ECML, and a large number of Eastern Region motive power duties had to be re-arranged to take account of the locomotive fleet being operated out of Immingham.

The Doncaster Division

Mention has just been made of a rather nebulous-sounding organisation known as the Doncaster division of the Eastern Region of British Railways; this was the geographical area within which all passenger and freight traffic was controlled from Gresley House, the control office built alongside the station concourse and opened during late 1960. At that time the office controlled approximately 220 route miles of track roughly bounded by Doncaster, Grantham, Mexborough, Gainsborough, Brocklesby and Kiveton. Only 16 collieries were included, which generated

some 2,250 wagons per day in and out of the area out of a total of 22,000 wagons handled daily amidst the total of over 750 freight workings. The Scunthorpe steelworks of Appleby-Frodingham and Richard Thomas & Baldwins provided the division's greatest amount of traffic by far, and BR was anxious to encourage the flow of raw materials and finished products. By 1962, BR was handling 90% of this traffic and the biggest problem was in finding enough new land in the area to provide new sidings and handling facilities — the steelworks were buying up space as fast as possible to ensure their own expansion. From the viewpoint of the early 1990s it is difficult to recall that barely 30 years previously the Scunthorpe steelworks were fed with home-produced raw iron ore (mined both locally and near Melton Mowbray) which was transported entirely by rail. The ore from Melton Mowbray was taken from the High Dyke branch to Scunthorpe via Sleaford, Boston, Louth and Grimsby, using the ECML for only a short stretch between Great Ponton and Barkston South Junction. Add to this the train-loads of coal, limestone and finished products all using the ex-GCR lines between Immingham, Scunthorpe and Doncaster and it is clearly seen why BR devoted so much effort to the steel industry; more trains passed Stainforth daily than the total amount of traffic using the ECML and the GN/GE Joint line.

If the division's steel traffic was looking in the pink of health in 1962, the same could certainly not be said for the area's coal business. Apart from that required by the steelworks, domestic consumption was decreasing, coal-fired gas plants were disappear-

Above:
**An eastbound train of empty oil tanks is hurried through
Barnby Dun by Class 31 locos Nos 31203 and 31185 on
13 December 1990.** *S. R. Batty*

ing fast and the merry-go-round era was years away
in the future. From moving out approximately 5,000
loaded wagons from 50 pits daily in 1955, the area
was lucky to handle half that number after only seven
years had passed. The remaining coal output still followed the same routes away from the town eastwards
to the Humber, and southwards to East Anglia and
London.

Traffic control at Gresley House was divided into
six areas: No 1, the South Yorkshire Joint Line; No 2,
from Waleswood Junction, Sheffield, to Wrawton
Junction; Barnetby; No 3, from Thorne Junction to
Brocklesby; No 4, from Thorne Junction to Denaby;
No 5, from Rossington on the ECML to Shaftholme
Junction, and No 6, from Rossington to Barkston
Junction near Grantham, including the GN/GE Joint
line to Gainsborough (Lea Road). During 1965 the
division was enlarged by taking over traffic control in
the Grantham area, which gave Doncaster a ruling
hand from Shaftholme to Stoke tunnel, from the
Humber to the Wash and from Mexborough to Melton
Mowbray. Revenue in the enlarged Division had
reached about £20 million by this time, including £7
million from coal produced at 18 pits and £5 million
from the three steel plants. Just over the horizon,
however, was the biggest bounty yet for the Division
— oil traffic. Massive refinery projects were being
planned for the Immingham area and BR had agreed
long-term contracts for the distribution of the products throughout the country. This new traffic was
expected to reach, by 1970, some 60 tank wagons to
be despatched daily; even in 1965 the division's daily
workload reached 5, 000 incoming wagons unloaded
and 3,500 loaded for despatch, creating a consistent
60-70% surplus of originating revenue over operating

costs. This was achieved through good use of
resources, and especially by means of block train
working, which did away with the shunting work
and standstill time involved with wagon-load traffic.
Not only was oil traffic threatening to fill up line
capacity on the ex-GCR lines, but coal traffic was
recovering and possible export traffic via Immingham
pointed towards improvements being needed beyond
Thorne towards Scunthorpe. Exporting of coal was
really the icing on the cake as far as coal haulage was
concerned — the real business lay with supplying the
CEGB's new power stations being built or planned for
the Trent and Aire valleys.

West Burton power station, near Retford, was England's first example of the merry-go-round system
being used between various pits and the power station, and two further projects were also planned for
the area; only Cottam ultimately came into use. Argu-
ments between BR and the NCB over who should pay
for the pit-head loading facility delayed the full
advantages of the mgr system from being realised for
years, but eventually the block trains of HOP-AB
wagons pulled Doncaster's coal traffic out of the dol-
drums and back into big business. Getting the mgr
system into full, effective operation took far longer
than it ever should have done, but even without this
new coal traffic the Doncaster division of the mid-
1960s was running at a very healthy profit — if the
entire BR system had even approached Doncaster's

profitability, BR's money problems would have disappeared completely. After the ER/NER merger of 1966, the division was enlarged even more from September 1970, when the former Hull division was absorbed.

The Plant: BREL and Beyond

During the mid-1960s, BR's workshop requirements were reviewed when the end of steam power was nigh and the maintenance activities were about to be altered radically. In 1964 a plan was made to spend £17 million to modernise various workshop facilities and improve working conditions, but this was to include some closures and reductions where deemed necessary. The foundry was closed, but generally the locomotive building and repair work was far less affected than the carriage and wagon side. A series of carriages was completed during 1958, and over the next three years several electric multiple-unit carriages were built in co-operation with York carriage works, but the 1962 Workshops Reorganisation Plan saw the end of all building and repair work during 1964. The main carriage shop was turned over to wagon repairs from 1965, when Carr wagon works was closed, and maintenance work on the diesel multiple-unit fleet was then carried out in the west carriage shop and the old north shed.

Diesel locomotive repair work was done at the Plant, particularly to Classes 20, 31, 37 and 40, but perhaps the most famous visitors of the entire diesel era were the Class 55 'Deltics'. These extremely powerful two-stroke machines were built by the English Electric Co from 1961 for service exclusively on the ECML, but the manufacturer was retained to supervise the maintenance and repair of the unusual twin power units until reliability was improved to a satisfactory level. By 1968 BR was ready to take over the entire maintenance effort, and the Plant — which had been involved with the 22-strong fleet through all its problems and tribulations over the past seven years — was given responsibility for engine overhaul work. A considerable amount of money was spent on tooling-up for working on the sophisticated engines, and the first overhaul was completed during December of that year. Work was transferred gradually from the Napier works, and Plant staff were given the necessary training by English Electric to allow the changeover to be fully completed by September 1969.

Great changes took place during 1970. Part of the 1968 Transport Act gave BR workshops the freedom to act as contractors and build or repair locomotives and rolling stock for non-BR customers. BR's workshop organisation totalled 14 sites employing 30,000 people and had a turnover of £100 million. From 1 January 1970 it became known as British Rail Engineering Ltd — BREL. The Plant was quick off the mark to exploit its new freedom, and soon had an order to build three Bo-Bo diesel locomotives for Northern Ireland Railways. This was the first such contract taken by a BREL works under the 1968 Act, and ended up at Doncaster in a rather roundabout way. Originally the contract was awarded to EE-AEI, but locomotive building at the Vulcan Foundry was brought to a sudden end with the GEC take-over of the EE-AEI combine. The job then went to the Leeds firm of the Hunslet Engine Co, which then found it had space limitations in its workshops and so subcontracted the work to the Plant.

Meanwhile locomotive overhaul work continued apace, especially in connection with the fitting of air brake equipment which was undertaken to eliminate vacuum-braked stock from the BR fleet. Even some of the AC electric locomotive fleet of Classes 83 and 84 were refurbished during the early 1970s. Locomotive building work recommenced in 1977 with a series of 85 locos of Class 56, but the story had strange beginnings rooted in the oil crises of the early 1970s. During 1973, BR was advised that due to expected shortages of oil and future price rises, it could expect the market for power station coal to increase dramatically within a relatively short time. The problem for BR was its lack of a suitable machine for hauling heavy coal trains over rather longer distances then it had been used to — although the Class 47 locos were doing a good job so far, they had very little power in reserve which could be used for hauling heavier train-loads. BR then cast around amongst the locomotive builders for a suitable product, and Brush Machines came up with the Class 56 scheme, based on their Class 47 design but fitted with a 3,250hp version of a proven English Electric engine and other suitable refinements. It then allocated construction of the 30 locomotives to a Romanian subsidiary company, which managed to deliver the first example by August 1976, the last being delivered some 12

months later. Unfortunately, the acceptance tests revealed a great deal of poor workmanship and faulty assembly, and the entire batch had to be rectified in various BR establishments. Construction of the Plant's batch, Nos 56031-115, started in late 1976, and the first loco was ready by April 1977. A total of five or six should have been in service by this time but delays had been caused by late delivery of parts from suppliers and the fabrication of certain structural parts in other BREL plants — this was brought about by a shortage of skilled men at Doncaster. The last machine was produced in January 1983, and the entire batch went into revenue-earning service straight from the Plant.

What was to be Doncaster's last exercise in locomotive building evolved during 1981, whilst the Class 56 assembly was under way. The recession-hit Railfreight sector needed a version of Class 56 which would be cheaper to build and maintain but which would still have the haulage ability of the earlier design. BREL produced its very own Class 58 design,

Below:
D3 bay in the main machine shop, 8 April 1957. *BR*

Right:
The DMU repair shop. *C. J. Marsden*

Below right:
The DMU repair shop during conversion to become part of the new Central Stores, pictured in October 1986. *C. J. Marsden*

using a modular construction which allowed cheaper
building costs and better access for maintenance
work, and a 12-cylinder 3,300hp version of the GEC-
Ruston engine. The first locomotive, No 58001,
emerged in November 1982, and the last, No 58050,
in April 1987. Although a capable machine, the ulti-
mate accolade of export orders has avoided the class
— BREL's hopes in this direction unfortunately did
not materialise. A further run of Class 58 was originally planned, but the order was cancelled after the
miners' strike of 1984-5 sent Railfreight's receipts
into a nosedive. In the midst of this disastrous dis-
pute, No 58020 was named *Doncaster Works BREL* on
7 November 1984.

Above:
Class 56 No. 56068 under construction, on 19 August 1979.
Brian Morrison

Right:
**Class 50 No 50041 *Bulwark* undergoes repair in No 4 bay on
20 November 1984, after being badly damaged during the
Paddington derailment of November 1983.** *C. J. Marsden*

using a modular construction which allowed cheaper
building costs and better access for maintenance
work, and a 12-cylinder 3,300hp version of the GEC-
Ruston engine. The first locomotive, No 58001,
emerged in November 1982, and the last, No 58050,
in April 1987. Although a capable machine, the ulti-
mate accolade of export orders has avoided the class
— BREL's hopes in this direction unfortunately did
not materialise. A further run of Class 58 was originally planned, but the order was cancelled after the
miners' strike of 1984-5 sent Railfreight's receipts
into a nosedive. In the midst of this disastrous dis-
pute, No 58020 was named *Doncaster Works BREL* on
7 November 1984.

Another English Electric-built class, the '50s',
proved regular visitors to the Plant from 1977, when
Doncaster took responsibility for maintenance of the
class. These were quite modern locomotives, dating
from 1967/68, but by the late 1970s several of their
high-tech features were causing problems with reliability and maintenance. By 1977 the mileage per
casualty was falling rapidly towards the unacceptably
low figure of 7,000; the fleet was then still in front-

line service on the West of England routes, and something had to be done. Therefore a refurbishment programme was drawn up and No 50006 was used as the
guinea pig; she emerged from the Plant on 14 November 1979, and the entire class was dealt with by late
1983. The miles per casualty figure climbed to 18-
20,000 by 1981 and the class was included in BR's
plans to 1994, when further overhauls would be due.
How circumstances change!

Soon after the last Class 58 locomotive had been
built the Plant was reorganised into a large stores and
repair depot under a BR scheme which effectively
ended any future possibility of locomotive building.

By the mid-1980s the maintenance requirements of the BR fleet had changed drastically. Locomotives were not as plentiful as in previous decades and the need for good utilisation meant that defective units could not be left abandoned at a remote depot awaiting a tow to a BREL works. The diesel multiple-unit fleet was changing from a largely 1950s-based collection of worn-out stock into a modern, 1980s fleet which was designed so that only small doses of simple maintenance would be needed, at longer service intervals. The BREL works at Crewe, Derby and York continued as centres for construction and heavy repair of all locomotives, multiple-units and coaching stock, and the works at Doncaster, Glasgow, Wolverton and Eastleigh came under the control of British Rail Maintenance Ltd (BRML) as 'level 5' depots.

The 'level' classification was applied also to the various traction and rolling stock maintenance depots (such as Leeds Neville Hill, where the ECML High-Speed Train fleet was maintained), and the actual classification referred to the facilities available. A Level 1 establishment would be simply a fuelling point; level 3 would allow light maintenance, such as 'B' and 'C' exams; and level 5 depots would perform all examinations and also carry out component exchange as well. Several depots around the country could perform level 5 tasks — such as power unit changes, body lifting — but the new scheme relied upon the availability of large items for component exchange which could be despatched quickly from stores to wherever required. Doncaster became the location of the new Central Store, where the routine movement of exchange spares was controlled and also where any component could be supplied on a 24hr emergency basis if needed. Thus the failed locos

which previously had to be dragged into, say, Crewe works could now be repaired at a local level 5 depot, where the necessary exchange parts could be delivered to allow a faster return to service. The Crimpsall became the largest of the BRML level 5 depots, and continued to work on the Class 31 heavy general overhaul programme during 1987/88 as well as undertake other heavy work on locomotives such as collision/fire damage, etc. The entire BR fleet of first generation DMUs was allocated for maintenance work, with the new Sprinter classes being absorbed as the older fleet was gradually replaced.

Wagon repair work prospered at the Plant, especially after the closure of the Shildon works in 1983. All types of vehicles were dealt with, but the fleet of merry-go-round coal wagons provided the bulk of the work. The shops were well-organised and well-equipped, and BR had made good investment in equipment and facilities to ensure the wagon fleet was kept in service as long as possible. In 1987 the wagon works took an early part in the privatisation programme which was slowly bearing down on BR; during the summer BR invited offers for the sale of the works, lock, stock and barrel and complete with all existing workload. A management buy-out was arranged and RFS Industries came into being on 16 October 1987, taking over 330,000sq ft of workshop space on a 22 acre site for a cost of £6 million. Apart from wagon overhaul, the works also undertook repair work to non-passenger rolling stock of all kinds, wheelsets, bogies and brake gear, but the initial objective was to reduce its dependence on BR work. After successfully tendering for the renewal of troublesome gearboxes on BR'S Pacer DMU stock, RFS secured an order in early 1988 for the overhaul

of the wagon fleet operated by the British Steel Corporation, at a value of £1 million. Plenty of BR business is available, but the company is going to great lengths to expand away from its traditional markets and find business in other engineering fields.

Local Passenger Services

The studies undertaken by the newly-established local passenger transport authorities in the mid-1970s reflected the needs of the areas concerned and proposed different solutions. Whereas the Leeds-based West Yorkshire PTE proposed a revival of the local rail network as part of the solution to the area's heavy commuter-based problems, the South Yorkshire PTE saw the diesel bus as the solution to most of its troubles. Apart from the heavily-populated areas of Sheffield, Rotherham and Barnsley, the SYPTE served relatively sparse areas which did not justify intense bus or train services. However, if a service fails to make the grade on one set of rules, it may well qualify under a different book. The Sheffield-Doncaster-Thorne-Hull and Cleethorpes service lay within the PTE's area as far as Thorne, and was a good revenue-producer between Sheffield and Doncaster. Traffic onwards was much quieter, but this was a Job Priority Area with relatively poor road communications which was deemed worthy of investment. The stations between Doncaster and Cleethorpes had been 'improved' some years previously, and the PTE eventually promised to support the line for a two-year period under Section 20 of the 1968 Transport Act. Because the PTE was essentially a bus-oriented organisation, and because the area had

a history of low loadings on local passenger services (only 1% of South Yorkshire public transport journeys were made by rail in the early 1970s), the PTE did not promote a policy of rolling stock renewal as happened in neighbouring West Yorkshire. The county did not even have a DMU depot within its boundary, and although a few vehicles were repainted into a SYPTE-styled livery for promotional purposes, the wide operating field of the first-generation DMUs made the idea a non-starter. The WYPTE hoped to share the cost of its own Class 141 DMU fleet with the SYPTE when the scheme was drawn up during 1982, but the initial cost and the design of the lightweight converted freight wagon chassis was not to the PTE's liking. Eventually these units did reach Doncaster, but this was done largely to get BR out of trouble when the ageing DMU fleet could not cope with the demands being made; the 141s would fill in with turns on a non-PTE supported service such as the lightly-used York-Selby-Doncaster run. By 1986 the better-riding and rather less troublesome Classes 142 and 144 had appeared, displacing the '141s' to other duties at the off-peak periods. The SYPTE was quite happy to use BR's own DMUs rather than get involved in a '141'-type saga as had happened in West Yorkshire, and the new Class 150 'Sprinters' would give a much better quality service on the longer runs such as the Sheffield-Hull/Cleethorpes services.

Under a series of timetable improvements made by BR during 1983 Doncaster became a focal point for main line traffic on both the East Coast and North-East/South-West services. The PTE services had been successfully revised and promoted during the previ-

Far left:
Class 58 locomotives under construction. *C. J. Marsden*

Above:
A two-car DMU empty stock working pauses for signals at Thorne North on 16 July 1990. *S. R. Batty*

Left:
A Class 156 Super Sprinter forming the 13.59 Sheffield-Hull passes Kirk Sandall on 3 December 1990. *S. R. Batty*

ous year to a point where loadings had improved by 45%, and BR's 1984 improvements to trackwork in the Swinton area allowed the local trains to use an extra two miles of faster line, giving an even better service. A new station was opened at Swinton, and a joint venture with the WYPTE saw stations opened during 1986 at Thurnscoe and at Goldthorpe, on the ex-Swinton & Knottingley line. This end of the York-Sheffield route had always been unsupported by the PTE, but the line offered a good route towards areas of employment and was seen as a benefit to the depressed Dearne Valley communities. Perhaps the PTE's new-found interest in rail activities was partly encouraged by the mayhem brought about by the de-

regulation of bus services which took place at this time!

Main Line Developments

Passenger facilities at Doncaster station were improved by a £112,000 modernisation scheme, which was approved in late 1974. This provided for a travel centre to be built at the north end of the concourse, on an area then used by the left luggage and other offices. Work started in March 1975 and was completed, at a cost of £125,000, in April 1976. The present passenger area is pleasant enough, with only the subway needing some smartening up.

A little-known passenger traffic closure took place during 1980, when the Adwick Junction-Stainforth Junction line passenger service was withdrawn from 13 September. This part of the ex-West Riding & Grimsby main line had seen only very infrequent passenger use during its entire life, consisting mainly of excursion traffic from Leeds to Cleethorpes, and the last scheduled service still surviving in 1980 was the summer only 08.26 (SO) Leeds-Cleethorpes; this ran until the end of the summer timetable, and in future years was diverted via Doncaster and thence to Gainsborough via the GN/GE Joint Line.

Mention has already been made of the 1984/85 timetable improvements made by BR. These were indirectly brought about by the recession of the early 1980s, when the 1981-planned Sheffield-Cudworth-Leeds resignalling scheme was cancelled during 1982, and the northern end of the ex-MR main line was abandoned for passenger traffic. Combined with this was a review of the utilisation of the High Speed Train fleet on the North-East/South-West service, resulting in trains for Newcastle and Scotland being diverted at Sheffield away from Leeds towards Doncaster. Leeds-bound traffic left Sheffield towards Wath Road and then took the S&K line to Moorthorpe, where the ex-WR&G line was joined for the run to Wakefield and Leeds. Doncaster thus became a crossroads for HST working, and the Sheffield line was improved to make way for the faster trains. Signalling from Mexborough East to the site of St James' station was improved to raise the line speed from 50mph to 70mph, except through Conisbrough tunnel where tight clearances would not allow any increase in speed. Physical problems such

as this prevented any greater speed increase being achieved at a reasonable cost. Cost also ruled out any alteration, at least for the time being, to the 25mph, three-quarters of a mile single-line approach to the station used by all Sheffield traffic; hope was expressed that this could be improved as part of the ECML electrification scheme which was being urgently pressed at the time.

Resignallinq and Electrification

BR's 1955 Modernisation Plan recognised that electrification was the only long-term traction option for the principal express-passenger carrying routes of the network. Choosing which routes to electrify required a considerable amount of crystal-ball gazing, and no mean amount of thought regarding the technical problems involved in converting a steam railway into one geared to the operation of equally heavy trains at much higher speeds and frequencies. As with all such railway projects, money was not exactly made readily available; and every proposal, scheme, rebuilding, alteration and almost every last length of rail had to be financially justified to the last percentage point. The two routes from London to Scotland were prime candidates even in the 1950s — the earliest ECML electrification proposals date back to the Edwardian era — but the West Coast route, with loops and branches to Northampton, Birmingham and Manchester, was the chosen line for the 25kV AC scheme. It was eventually completed through to Glasgow in 1974 after years of delay caused by 'stop-go' investment policies.

Above left:
Class 307 EMU No 307120 passes Hampole with the 11.39 Doncaster-Leeds on a misty 14 December 1990. *S. R. Batty*

Above:
A pair of Class 20 locos, Nos 20069 and 20095, take a Lackenby-Corby steel coil train along the avoiding line near Hexthorpe Junction on 14 January 1991. *S. R. Batty*

Right:
Doncaster's new travel centre, opened on 7 April 1976. This end of the station was further rebuilt during 1990/91. *BR*

The ECML served fewer centres of population and industry compared to the West Coast route, but, just as in the days of Hudson and Denison, this feature gave the route its greatest asset — the potential for prolonged high-speed haulage. The 'Deltic' era hammered home this point with considerable vigour: although destined to rely on diesel propulsion for an unknown period, BR used the most advanced motive power available to keep on cutting away at schedules and running ever-faster trains. Passenger traffic between the North-East and King's Cross was particularly lucrative, but serious competition from air traffic emerged in the late 1960s/early 1970s and the

expanding motorway network posed a threat to the West Riding services. Journey times had to be reduced even further, and this was done by a rolling programme of resignalling (together with alterations to trackwork and civil engineering), the High Speed Train fleet, and, ultimately, electrification.

The ECML resignalling scheme was started during 1969, when a £2 million scheme for work between King's Cross and Newcastle was first proposed. Approval for work as far north as Sandy was approved late in 1970. By early 1972 outline schemes had been laid for work as far as Doncaster, but nothing was expected to be seen here before 1976. The

A Leeds-King's Cross HST enters the station as Class 55 No 55017 arrives at Marshgate Junction with the 16.30 Hull-King's Cross on 10 April 1981. The realigned Leeds lines can be clearly seen on the left. *L. A. Nixon*

Peterborough scheme was expected to be completed in two stages by 1975, and the Doncaster scheme would ultimately cover the ECML from Stoke tunnel to Shaftholme Junction. Multiple aspect colour light signalling was already in operation from Doncaster to Berwick-upon-Tweed; when eventually sanctioned and completed, the Doncaster resignalling would eliminate semaphore operation from the English section of the East Coast main line.

Approval was eventually obtained during the summer of 1974, covering a £25 million track and MAS plan reaching along 84 miles of the ECML from milepost 101, just outside the northern portal of Stoke tunnel, to milepost 185 near Naburn, south of York. The new signalling centre to be built south of Doncaster station would replace 51 mechanical boxes and completion was expected by 1977, when (hopefully) the new HST fleet would be able to reduce journey times to Newcastle to 3hr, Edinburgh to 4hr 30min and Leeds to 2hr 15min. The new signalling equipment was installed with future electrification very much in mind, and the civil engineering work would see 250 of the 268 miles from King's Cross to Newcastle uprated for 125mph running. At Doncaster the line limit for through traffic was to be raised from 60mph to no less than 105mph, and the former Dearne Valley viaduct over the ECML at Black Carr was to be used as a flyover to carry the GN/GE Joint line traffic clear of the main line.

Work progressed slowly due to the large amount of work involved; signalling via two-, three- and four-aspect equipment was used on lines which varied in usage from mineral-only to full ECML standard. Whereas the Peterborough scheme was a modestly-sized exercise covering little more than a straight high-speed main line, the Doncaster plan covered a much larger area which contained many junctions and routes carrying a wide variety of traffic. The last semaphore signal on the entire ECML was taken out of service on 21 September 1978 when Doncaster's

Decoy No 2 signalbox up home signal was removed and handed over to the ER General Manager, Mr Frank Patterson, who then passed it on to the National Railway Museum. Track relaying in the station area from 4 March to 8 April 1979 saw the alteration of Marshgate Junction, and some unusual diversions were operated during this period; some Leeds trains ran via Selby or out to Stainforth before reversing back along the WR&G towards Adwick and Wakefield, and some Wakefield traffic ran via Askern and Knottingley with a few trains travelling via Selby and Leeds to reach Westgate from the northern approach.

The first stage of the power box was brought into use during July 1979, and control was extended as far as Stoke, at the Peterborough area boundary, on 3 February 1980. The official opening was carried out by Sir Peter Parker on 8 December 1981, some three years after the original completion date had been delayed by pressure on investment cash. The scheme had cost £40 million, the same in real terms as the 1974 figure of £25 million, and had replaced 52 old signalboxes and 11 gateboxes over a total of 155 route miles. The boundaries along the ECML were also slightly different from those originally planned, and reached from MP 100 (at the south end of Stoke tunnel) to MP 163 on the down line at Moss level crossing and to MP 169 on the up line, just south of Temple Hirst Junction.

At the same time as the southern end of the ECML was being resignalled, BR was pressing ahead with schemes for electrifying the lines to Leeds and Newcastle. The diesel HST fleet was in full ECML service from May 1979 and was an immediate success with the travelling public — so successful that severe overcrowding became a problem. Diesel power was but a stop-gap answer, and only full electrification could provide the speeds and frequencies required on the 400-mile run from London to Edinburgh. Once again, the problem was in convincing governments that the

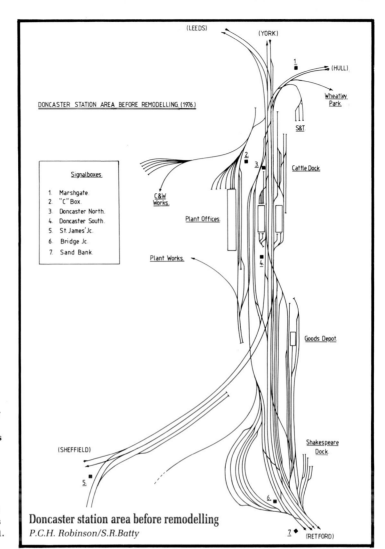

DONCASTER STATION AREA BEFORE REMODELLING. (1976.)

(LEEDS)

(YORK)

1 ■   → (HULL)

Wheatley Park.

S&T.

Signalboxes.

1. Marshgate.
2. "C" Box.
3. Doncaster North.
4. Doncaster South.
5. St. James' Jc.
6. Bridge Jc.
7. Sand Bank.

2 ■
3 ■

Cattle Dock.

C&W Works.

Plant Offices.

Plant Works.

4 ■

Goods Depot.

Shakespeare Dock.

(SHEFFIELD)

5 ■

Doncaster station area before remodelling
P.C.H. Robinson/S.R.Batty

6 ■

7 ◆   (RETFORD)

Below left:
Class 47 No 47413 prepares to draw the 09.10 King's Cross-Leeds out of the station on 7 January 1991. Leeds trains were being diverted via Normanton due to a landslip near Ardsley tunnel. *S. R. Batty*

Below:
Driving Van Trailer No 82205 leads the way with the 14.10 Leeds-King's Cross at Bentley on 14 January 1991. *S. R. Batty*

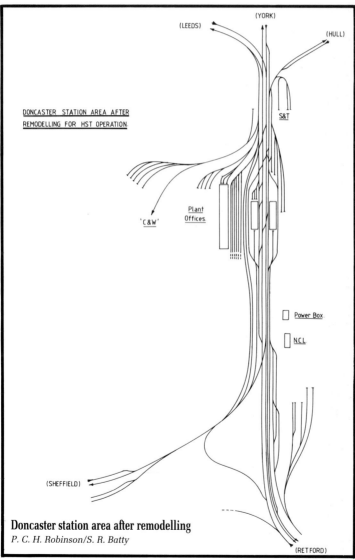

DONCASTER STATION AREA AFTER REMODELLING FOR HST OPERATION.

(YORK)

(LEEDS)

(HULL)

S&T

Plant Offices.

'C&W'

Power Box.

N.C.L

(SHEFFIELD)

(RETFORD)

Doncaster station area after remodelling
P. C. H. Robinson/S. R. Batty

returns would justify the expenditure. In 1978, a joint BR/Department of Transport paper placed the ECML at the top of the electrification list, but four years passed before the Department finally made any approving noises at all towards BR. By then the recession of the early 1980s had hit hard and changed the business picture of ECML traffic levels, forcing BR to draw up a revised justification which included running the wires through from Newcastle to Edinburgh. (Earlier plans to use diesel traction over this stretch of line were found, after practical tests, to involve difficult shunting work at Newcastle Central station, a time penalty, and the risk of alienating some of the ECML's best customers from north of the border.) Despite having a definite anti-rail bias in matters of transport policy, the government announced the authorisation of the full scheme on 27 July 1984. BR was to be allowed to spend £306 million of its own money, including £170 million on infrastructure, £62 million on motive power and £74 million on rolling stock — and the scheme was to reach Leeds by October 1989 and Edinburgh by May 1991.

Work went ahead rapidly, starting from the outermost point of the Great Northern electrification scheme at Hitchin and allowing energisation to Huntingdon during the autumn of 1987. Power was switched on to Peascliffe during March 1988 and through Doncaster to Leeds during April, some 18 months ahead of the original estimated completion date. The solitary Brush-built Class 89 Co-Co locomotive, No 89001, became a regular visitor on crew-training runs, and later gave sterling service on passenger duties until sufficient numbers of the GEC-built Class 91 machines were available. The first electric locomotive worked into Leeds on 11 August 1988, when Class 91 No 91004 arrived with a test coach, six sleeping cars and HST power car No 43014 bringing up the rear. Electric haulage took over as the availability of locomotives allowed; No 89001 regularly worked to Leeds from late 1988 but it was March of 1989 before any regular Class 91 duties appeared.

Energisation from Arksey to Copmanthorpe took place on 3 July 1989 and was extended into York station during the autumn; occasional electric haulage of passenger trains commenced with the winter 1989/1990 timetable. At the time of writing, full electric operation to Newcastle and Edinburgh is not expected to take place before July 1991, due to the extent of the 'Clapham' modification work needed in the Newcastle resignalling scheme.

An unexpected development has been the early deployment of electric multiple-units on the Leeds line. Problems with the DMU fleet in West Yorkshire prompted the PTE to urge BR to provide some extra rolling stock to ease the daily round of overcrowding and late-running or cancelled trains. The quickest answer was to send a batch of Class 307 four-car units which were displaced from the Liverpool Street-Southend service during the summer of 1989; six units, complete with Network SouthEast livery, were despatched and entered service during September 1990. Repainting into West Yorkshire red and cream paintwork was done gradually, and after one or two hiccups the units settled down and allowed the release of DMUs on to other parts of the WYPTE system. Plans exist for considerable electrification work in West Yorkshire, but at the moment pressure of work on BR's staff is expected to delay any new work until 1995 at least. Beyond that date, brand-new EMU stock may reach Doncaster from Leeds and Wakefield.

So much for Doncaster's railway development over the past 150 years! Changes over more recent decades have altered the railway picture greatly, but compared to many centres which have either been reduced to a shadow of their former selves or destroyed completely, Doncaster has survived remarkably well. The Barnsley coalfield has virtually disappeared and the Doncaster field is somewhat reduced, but the power station coal traffic is very healthy (at least for the present) and provides a lucrative business. Of the collieries, some have disappeared (Yorkshire Main, Denaby, Cadeby, Firbeck,

Bullcroft, Brodsworth), some survive (Rossington, Markham Main, Askern, Bentley) and some prosper (Maltby, Harworth). Many of the railways which shared their prosperity with the pits have gone too — virtually no trace remains of the Hull & Barnsley, the H&BR/GCR Joint or the Dearne Valley Railway — but the South Yorkshire Joint quietly prospers and will presumably continue to do so as long as the coal traffic holds up. The East Coast main line has always been a money-spinner and will continue to provide a healthy income for BR as long as investment in BR's best motive power, rolling stock and infrastructure is allowed to progress. Local passenger services to Leeds, Sheffield, Hull and Cleethorpes should benefit from the spin-off effect of the WYPTE's dedication to using the rail network to the full, and from the introduction of better 'Sprinter' class stock on the SYPTE-sponsored routes. The only long shadows are falling on the lightly-used services to Selby and York and to Gainsborough and Spalding via the GN/GE Joint line.

And what of the Plant? After being organised, re-organised, privatised and rationalised, it too is still in business but in a different form. The demands of BR and the changing nature of rolling stock and motive power fleets have seen the end of building work and a concentration on maintenance activity and spares inventory needs, but the Plant still fulfils an urgent requirement in keeping the wheels turning. RFS Industries is keen to take on a great variety of work, and could perhaps start a new line of wagon building which would continue, in some fashion, from where BR left off. There should be enough activity on the entire site to allow a celebration of the Plant's 150th year in business — it's not *that* far away!

Locomotive Allocations

1947

CLASS A3 4-6-2

48 *Doncaster*   49 *Galtee More*   58 *Blair Athol*
63 *Isinglass*   103 *Flying Scotsman*

CLASS A2/3 4-6-2

520 *Owen Tudor*

CLASS A2 4-6-2

525 *A. H. Peppercorn*

CLASS V2 2-6-2

815,	826,	830-32,	845,	846,	849,
852,	857,	861,	867,	870,	872,
875,	877,	880,	881,	889,	890,
896,	902,	906,	917,	928,	930,
935,	943,	948,	956.		

CLASS Bl 4-6-0

1026,	1120,	1124-27,	1170,	1190,	1191,
1193,	1194,	1196,	1201,		

1246 *Lord Balfour of Burleigh*   1247 *Lord Burghley*
1248 *Geoffrey Gibbs*   1249 *Fitzherbert Wright*
1250 *A. Harold Bibby*   1265

CLASS K3 2-6-0

1856,	1860,	1907,	1910,	1918,	1978.

CLASS Cl 4-4-2

2854,   2877,   2885.

CLASS 04 2-8-0

3572,	3586,	3587,	3593,	3594,	3598,
3600,	3601,	3607,	3616,	3617,	3621,
3623,	3624,	3727,	3643,	3647,	3657,
3659,	3660,	3668,	3671,	3682,	3684,
3693,	3697,	3698,	3719,	3728,	3731,
3738,	3741,	3745,	3757,	3758,	3765,
3800,	3832,	3847,	3864,	3883,	3884,
3891,	3900,	3911,	3915.		

CLASS 02 2-8-0

3976-8

CLASS J6 0-6-0

4179,	4183,	4185,	4193,	4195,	4209,
4218,	4219,	4232,	4236,	4241,	4243,
4255,	4258,	4259,	4261-64,	4270,	4279.

CLASS J39 0-6-0

4713,	4721,	4737,	4758,	4835,	4885,
4891,	4893,	4902,	4909,	4910,	4951,
4952,	4967,	4976,	4977,	4984.	

CLASS J55 0-6-0T

8317.

CLASS J52 0-6-0T

8763,	8769,	8775,	8786,	8800,	8804,
8806,	8813,	8835-37,	8841-47,	8849,	
8857,	8860,	8865,	8869,	8870,	8885,
8886,	8890,	8893,	8899.		

CLASS J50 0-6-0T

8918,	8926,	8936,	8974,	8979,	8980,
8985-89,	8991				

TOTAL = 194.

Below:
**Brush Type 2 No 5802 awaits departure from Doncaster in
April 1969 with the 12.00 Newcastle-Lincoln service.**
Leslie Riley

1959

CLASS A3 4-6-2
60046 *Diamond Jubilee*   60064 *Tagalie*   60067 *Ladas*
60102 *Sir Frederick Banbury*   60104 *Solario*   60108 *Gay Crusader*
60112 *St Simon*

CLASS Al 4-6-2
60113 *Great Northern*   60114 *W.P. Allen*   60119 *Patrick Stirling*
60122 *Curlew*   60125 *Scottish Union*   60128 *Bongrace*
60136 *Alcazar*   60139 *Sea Eagle*   60144 *Kings Courier*
60149 *Amadis*   60156 *Great Central*   60157 *Great Eastern*
60158 *Aberdonian*

CLASS Wl 4-6-4
60700.

CLASS V2 2-6-2
60817,   60841,   60849   60852,   60857,   60866
60870,   60872 *King's Own Yorkshire Light Infantry*
60880,   60881,   60889,   60896,   60899,   60905,
60909,   60917,   60921,   60928,   60930,   60935,
60936,   60943,   60956.

CLASS Bl 4-6-0
61036   *Ralph Assheton*   61087,   61107,   61114,
61120,   61121,   61122,   61124,   61125,   61127,
61128,   61145,   61155,   61157,   61158,   61170,
61193,   61196,   61213,   61225,   61247   *Lord Burghley*
61250, *A. Harold Bibby*   61266,   61285,   61326,   61365,
61377.

CLASS K3 2-6-0
61800,   61803,   61812,   61829,   61887,   61895,
61925,   61940,   61961,   61964.

CLASS 04 2-8-0
63613,   63618,   63677,   63693,   63698,   63858.

CLASS 02 2-8-0
63922,   63928,   63934,   63935,   63939,
63941,   63942,   63943,   63951-58,   63962-64,
63967-69,   63973-75,   63977,   63978,
63981,   63983-85.

CLASS J6 0-6-0
64179,   64185,   64209,   64232,   64241,
64258,   64259,   64270.

CLASS J39 0-6-0
64716,   64721-23,   64737,   64810,   64827,
64838,   64874,   64876,   64883,   64885,
64909,   64967,   64972,   64981,   64987.

CLASS J94 0-6-0ST
68020,   68022,   68069,   68071.

CLASS J69 0-6-0T
68498,   68502,   68507,   68508,   68520,
68530,   68556,   68558,   68569,   68587,
68621.

CLASS J68 0-6-0T
68654.

CLASS J50 0-6-0T
68962,   68964,   68965,   68973.

CLASS WD 2-8-0
90108,   90144,   90255,   90453,   90537,
90538,   90550,   90569,   90602,   90636,
90696   90732 *Vulcan*

CLASS 9F 2-10-0
92168-77,   92189,   92191,   92192,   92199,
92200,   92201.

TOTAL =191.

Above:
The Leeds-bound portion of the 09.10 King's Cross-Leeds/Hull leaves Doncaster behind Class 47/4 No 47411 on 4 July 1975. *J. E. Oxley*

1965

CLASS B1 4-6-0
61039   *Steinbok*,   61050,   61051,   61055,
61058,   61087,   61093,   61107,   61121,   61127,   61157,
61158,   61196,   61208,   61225,   61326,   61329,   61348,
61360,   61367,   61384.

CLASS 04 2-8-0
63593,   63613,   63688,   63730,   63734,   63738,
63764,   63785,   63818,   63858.

CLASS WD 2-8-0
90001,   90018,   90063,   90073,   90096,   90154,
90156,   90158,   90169,   90195,   90203,   90211,
90235,   90252,   90255,   90277,   90279,   90293,
90296,   90305,   90330,   90364,   90365,   90369,
90372,   90421,   90428,   90448,   90476,   90477,
90480,   90484,   90498,   90506,   90538,   90557,
90569,   90580,   90636,   90675,   90683,   90687,
90709,   90718.

CLASS 9F 2-10-0
92168,   92172,   92174,   92183,   92190,   92201.

BR Diesel-Electric 0-6-0 Shunters
D3473, D3474, D3479-84
D3621-23, D3637, D3649-51,
D4078-82.

TOTAL = 101